NATIONAL DEFENSE RESE

T0288593

Diversity Leadership in the U.S. Department of Defense

Analysis of the Key Roles, Responsibilities, and Attributes of Diversity Leaders

Maria C. Lytell, Kirsten M. Keller, Beth Katz,
Jefferson P. Marquis, Jerry M. Sollinger

Prepared for the Office of the Secretary of Defense

For more information on this publication, visit www.rand.org/t/rr1148

Library of Congress Cataloging-in-Publication Data

ISBN: 978-0-8330-9270-0

Published by the RAND Corporation, Santa Monica, Calif.

© Copyright 2016 RAND Corporation

RAND® is a registered trademark.

Cover image courtesy of Kamaga/Fotolia.

Support RAND
Make a tax-deductible charitable contribution at
www.rand.org/giving/contribute

www.rand.org

Preface

In August of 2011, President Barack Obama issued Executive Order 13583: "Establishing a Coordinated Government-Wide Initiative to Promote Diversity and Inclusion in the Federal Workforce." In 2012, the U.S. Department of Defense (DoD) published a strategic plan to carry out the President's directive. The purpose of this study was to help DoD identify the knowledge, skills, abilities, and other personal characteristics needed in those individuals who will be responsible for implementing strategic diversity plans in DoD components and other strategic diversity and inclusion initiatives. The project analyzed relevant leadership positions in diversity management (also known as diversity and inclusion) and examined practices identified by diversity experts in industry, the public sector (including DoD), and academia. This report should interest policymakers and others concerned with requirements for leaders of strategic-level diversity and inclusion policies and programs.

This research was sponsored by the Office of Diversity Management and Equal Opportunity in the Office of the Under Secretary of Defense (Personnel and Readiness) and conducted within the Forces and Resources Policy Center of the RAND National Defense Research Institute, a federally funded research and development center sponsored by the Office of the Secretary of Defense, the Joint Staff, the Unified Combatant Commands, the Navy, the Marine Corps, the defense agencies, and the defense Intelligence Community. For more information on the Forces and Resources Policy Center, see www.rand.org/nsrd/ndri/centers/frp or contact the director (contact information is provided on the web page).

Contents

Preface iii
Tables vii
Summary ix
Acknowledgments xxi
Abbreviations xxiii

CHAPTER ONE
Introduction 1
Study Questions and Approach 2
Organization of This Report 11

CHAPTER TWO
Roles and Responsibilities for Diversity Leaders 13
Views on Roles and Responsibilities for Diversity Leaders 14
Proposals for Structuring a Diversity Office in DoD 26
Summary 30

CHAPTER THREE
KSAOs for Diversity Leaders 33
KSAOs Identified by Diversity Leaders 33
Summary 47

CHAPTER FOUR
Selection and Development of KSAOs for Diversity Leaders 49
Leadership KSAOs by Organizational Level 50
Malleability of Leadership KSAOs 51

Professional Development for Diversity Leaders 59
Diversity Education Programs at Higher-Education Institutions 65
Summary.. 67

CHAPTER FIVE
Conclusions and Recommendations 69
Several KSAOs Are Preferred or Required to Perform Diversity
    Leader Roles and Responsibilities.. 70
Some KSAOs Can Be Improved Through Training and Education 72
DoD Should Determine Training and Education Requirements for
    Diversity Leader Positions.. 73
Final Remarks 78

APPENDIXES
A. Methodology 81
B. Job Posting and Interview Coding and Results...................... 93
C. Diversity Education Programs 137

References 149

Tables

S.1.   Conclusions About Development Potential of KSAOs
for Future Diversity Leaders...................................... xvi
1.1.   Definitions of Key Diversity-Related Terms...................... 3
2.1.   Roles and Responsibilities for Diversity Leaders Identified
by Interviewees.. 15
3.1.   KSAOs for Diversity Leaders as Identified by Interviewees ... 34
4.1.   Overview of Domain Model of (Managerial)
Competencies 52
4.2.   Conclusions About Development Potential of KSAOs
for Future Diversity Leaders...................................... 60
A.1.   Competency Models for Diversity Leadership 83
B.1.   Job Postings Codes—Industry and Job Title.................... 94
B.2.   Job Postings Results—Industry and Job Title 95
B.3.   Job Postings Codes—Organizational Relationships 95
B.4.   Job Postings Results—Organizational Relationships 96
B.5.   Job Postings Codes—Work Experience........................ 97
B.6.   Job Postings Results—Work Experience........................ 97
B.7.   Job Postings Codes—Education and Training
Background... 98
B.8.   Job Postings Results—Education and Training
Background... 99
B.9.   Job Postings Codes—Diversity Leader Roles and
Responsibilities.. 100
B.10.   Job Postings Results—Diversity Leader Roles and
Responsibilities.. 102
B.11.   Job Postings Codes—KSAOs 104
B.12.   Job Postings Results—KSAOs 108

B.13.   Non-DoD Interview Results—Industry and Job Title........ 111
B.14.   Non-DoD Interview Results—Position Tenure................ 112
B.15.   Non-DoD Interview Results—Organization Tenure......... 112
B.16.   Non-DoD Interview Results—Reporting Chain.............. 113
B.17.   Non-DoD Interview Codes—Office Structure................ 113
B.18.   Non-DoD Interview Results—Office Structure, Staff,
         and Budget 114
B.19.   Non-DoD Interview Codes—Prior Work Experience........ 115
B.20.   Non-DoD Interview Results—Prior Work Experience....... 116
B.21.   Non-DoD Interview Codes—Education and Training
         Background.. 117
B.22.   Non-DoD Interview Results—Education and Training
         Background.. 118
B.23.   Non-DoD Interview Codes—Diversity Strategy and
         Goals 119
B.24.   Non-DoD Interview Results—Diversity Strategy and
         Goals 120
B.25.   Non-DoD Interview Codes—Definitions of Diversity,
         EEO, and Related Terms 121
B.26.   Non-DoD Interview Results—Definitions of Diversity,
         EEO, and Related Terms 123
B.27.   Non-DoD Interview Codes—Staff Roles and
         Responsibilities... 124
B.28.   Non-DoD Interview Results—Staff Roles and
         Responsibilities... 125
B.29.   Non-DoD Interview Codes—Diversity Leader Roles and
         Responsibilities... 126
B.30.   Non-DoD Interview Results—Diversity Leader Roles
         and Responsibilities.. 129
B.31.   Non-DoD Interview Codes—KSAOs 130
B.32.   Non-DoD Interview Results—KSAOs 134
B.33.   DoD Interview Codes—Position and Organizational
         Structure.. 136
C.1.   Program Characteristics....................................... 140
C.2.   Course Topics and Descriptions 143

Summary

Background and Purpose

In August of 2011, President Barack Obama issued an Executive Order directing a government-wide initiative to promote diversity and inclusion (D&I) in the federal workforce (White House, 2011). One part of that Executive Order charged each federal department and agency to develop a strategic plan for promoting a diverse and inclusive workforce. In response, the U.S. Department of Defense (DoD) published its D&I strategic plan, which established the following three goals:

1. Ensure leadership commitment to an accountable and sustained diversity effort.
2. Employ an aligned strategic outreach effort to identify, attract, and recruit from a broad talent pool reflective of the nation DoD serves.
3. Develop, mentor, and retain top talent from across the total force (DoD, 2012).

The various DoD components have built or are building their D&I plans. As DoD components move forward with implementation of their plans, they will have to determine what type of leader is required, including the attributes and experiences that best suit leaders to implement D&I programs. To help DoD in its efforts, the Office of Diversity Management and Equal Opportunity (ODMEO) asked RAND to identify the key attributes and experiences needed by its *diversity leaders*—i.e., the individuals who will be primarily responsible for implementation of D&I plans in DoD. This report responds to that request, and addresses the following three questions:

1. What should the key requirements for the position of a DoD diversity leader be?
2. What attributes and experiences may be needed to perform those requirements?
3. What would DoD need to do to develop its future diversity leaders?

Our Approach

To address the three study questions, we collected, reviewed, and analyzed information from several sources. Our primary source of information was interviews with 16 diversity and equal employment opportunity/military equal opportunity (EEO/MEO) leaders, as well as other senior leaders, across DoD components, and interviews with 47 senior-level diversity leaders (e.g., chief diversity officers [CDOs]) from private-sector and public-sector organizations. The primary goal of the DoD interviews was to address the first question about key requirements for DoD diversity leaders. The interview questions focused on future positions because we wished to determine what the requirements for DoD leader positions *should* be, not what the requirements are currently. The primary goal of interviews with diversity leaders outside DoD (i.e., non-DoD interviews) was to identify attributes— namely, knowledge, skills, abilities, and other personal characteristics (KSAOs)—and experiences that may be needed by diversity leaders. Because the diversity leader position is still evolving in DoD, we elicited insights from diversity leaders across a variety of organizations and industries. We integrated our findings from the two interview sources to identify key roles, responsibilities, KSAOs, and experiences for DoD diversity leaders.

Although we integrated the interview findings, we analyzed the content of the two main interview sources separately because of differences in question framing (i.e., future-oriented for DoD interviews versus present-oriented for non-DoD interviews). We also conducted two sets of secondary analyses to identify differences between groups within the two interview samples, as follows:

- non-DoD interviewees from for-profit organizations (n = 25 for roles/responsibilities; n = 26 for KSAOs) versus non-DoD interviewees from not-for-profit organizations (n = 20 for roles/responsibilities; n = 21 for KSAOs)
- senior-level DoD leaders (n = 6) versus DoD diversity and EEO/MEO leaders (n = 10).

Our findings reflect main themes from both sets of interviews, but we note places where differences based on our secondary analyses arise.

To supplement our interview findings, we also gathered information from job postings for senior diversity leaders, the scientific literature, and a review of diversity education programs. Specifically, we content-analyzed 53 online postings for senior diversity leadership positions to identify desired and required roles, responsibilities, KSAOs, and experiences (e.g., training, education). We also reviewed research and practitioner literature to identify diversity leader KSAOs or competencies. We supplemented this literature search with research literature on general management and leadership KSAOs. Finally, to supplement our interview findings regarding training and education for diversity leaders, we content-analyzed a convenience sample of nine diversity education programs across six higher-education institutions.

Despite using multiple sources to address our three study questions, our approach is not without limitations. A main limitation for our study—and for many studies on diversity leadership KSAOs or competencies—is that it relies primarily on the perspectives of individuals currently working in the area of D&I. We did not empirically validate these KSAOs against diversity leaders' performance or other important organizational outcomes. The D&I field as a whole faces this limitation because an agreed-upon set of KSAOs has not been identified. Nonetheless, we believe that our study's strength comes from the multiple perspectives offered by our different sources and the tailoring of the training and education discussion to the needs of DoD.

To Perform Diversity Leader Roles and Responsibilities, Certain Knowledge, Skills, Abilities, and Other Personal Characteristics Are Either Required or Preferred

Based on our interviews with diversity leaders, both in DoD and in organizations outside DoD, and on what we gleaned from online job postings and the literature, we identified the following categories of key roles and responsibilities:

- strategic leadership (including leading diversity programs/initiatives)
- stakeholder engagement
- tracking diversity trends
- human resources–related (HR-related) activities.

The order of the categories roughly reflects the importance accorded to the roles by diversity leaders outside DoD.[1] Thus, strategic leadership and stakeholder engagement ranked as particularly important for those who spearhead diversity efforts. These categories include such activities as advising the organization's top leadership and educating its workforce on diversity goals, plans, and initiatives. However, the categories also have an external focus to include working with suppliers, local communities, and other external stakeholders to ensure that the organization's diversity message is promulgated, as well as developing and communicating a D&I vision. Tracking diversity is less critical but still important as a way for diversity leaders to benchmark their initiatives and to demonstrate a return on the investments made in promoting diversity. Tracking such trends also helps diversity leaders to forecast workforce changes that their organization needs to adapt

---

[1]   As we explain later in the report, we use our non-DoD diversity leader results to organize results because they reflect a larger sample. However, we show results from our DoD interviews so that readers can note differences between the two samples.

in terms of attracting and retaining talent. Diversity leaders also work with or within HR departments to provide perspective for recruiting, hiring, and development practices.

To carry out the responsibilities within these categories, diversity leaders would ideally have the categories of KSAOs listed below:

- interpersonal skills
- business expertise
- leadership skills
- EEO/MEO, affirmative action (AA), and diversity knowledge and skill
- personality and attitudes: driven personality and commitment to diversity
- analytical abilities and skills
- critical thinking and problem-solving skills
- multicultural competence.

Those we interviewed most often mentioned interpersonal skills. Many diversity leaders are not in charge of any of the core/operational business units in their organizations and therefore need interpersonal skills to communicate and forge relationships with people across the organization to gain the "buy-in" needed to implement D&I strategies. They also need these skills to project an image of the organization as one that values diversity. Such a strategic message can help attract diverse talent, suppliers, and customers.

Many diversity leaders run programs or offices, a responsibility that involves budgets and staffs. Thus, to be effective, they need both leadership skills and business expertise. Business expertise includes both technical knowledge and skills related to business activities (e.g., how to recruit a diverse applicant pool), as well as knowledge about how the organizations' core business units operate. In our interviews, corporate diversity leaders made more mention of core business knowledge than DoD and other not-for-profit diversity leaders did. The corporate versus non-corporate distinction might reflect a corporate diversity leader's need to engage with internal stakeholders and to be able to link diversity efforts to the company's branding strategy. In contrast, not-for-profit diversity leaders made more mention of leadership skills and EEO/MEO, AA, and diversity knowledge and skills than corporate diversity leaders did. The leadership skill differences were affected by greater mention of general leadership skills (e.g., managing personnel and budgets) among not-for-profit leaders. A likely explanation for differences in responses regarding EEO/MEO, AA, and diversity knowledge and skills is that the not-for-profit leaders in our interview sample have more EEO responsibilities than the corporate leaders.

Regardless of organizational type, diversity leaders will also benefit from certain personality characteristics and attitudes. Based on what we heard in our interviews and saw in the job postings, being driven or persistent was considered important. Often, diversity leaders find themselves trying to change organizations, sometimes in fundamental ways. At times they cope with simple bureaucratic inertia; other times they encounter active resistance. In either case, success demands persistence. Diversity leaders also need the ability to develop and understand diversity metrics to track diversity trends, although DoD senior leaders did not mention analytical ability and skills. In contrast, six of the ten DoD diversity and EEO/MEO leaders mentioned these skills as needed by diversity leaders. We surmise that senior leaders are further removed from the activities required to identify and report diversity trends, whereas diversity and EEO/MEO leaders are responsible for these activities and, therefore, cite them.

Although our interviewees did not mention critical thinking skills and problem-solving skills, the literature on leadership KSAOs argues that leaders need these skills to deal with the complexities of organizational issues they address, such as promoting organizational change initiatives that foster D&I. Leaders—especially diversity leaders—also require multicultural competence to promote opportunities for greater D&I in their organizations.

Based on our review of the literature on leadership KSAOs, we identified many of the diversity leader KSAOs as those needed by different types of organizational leaders. However, diversity leaders might need certain KSAOs (e.g., multicultural competence) at higher levels than other types of organizational leaders.

Some KSAOs Can Be Improved Through Training and Education

Some attributes of effective diversity leaders can be enhanced or developed; others less so. One model of managerial competencies reviewed for this project proposes a four-domain taxonomy (see Hogan and Warrenfeltz, 2003; Hogan and Kaiser, 2005). The four domains—intrapersonal, interpersonal, leadership, and business—represent a hierarchy of trainability. Intrapersonal KSAOs are the hardest to train, and the business ones are the easiest. The implications are that the intrapersonal KSAOs should form the basis of selection of diversity leaders, and those in the business domain can then be (further) developed. Similar efforts to identify malleable or "developable" leadership KSAOs are found in literature on developmental assessment centers (DACs), which are interventions designed to develop individuals for managerial or leadership positions. Thornton and Rupp (2005) rate the difficulty of developing a sample of leadership KSAOs to help practitioners identify the types of KSAOs to include in DACs. Like Hogan and colleagues, Thornton and Rupp rate personality characteristics as "very difficult to develop" and rate interpersonal skills and leadership skills as "difficult to develop." Overall, the literature on the developability or malleability of managerial competencies/KSAOs suggests that personality and motivation are very difficult to develop; interpersonal skills and leadership skills difficult to develop; and skills related to problem-solving, communication, and technical skills (e.g., business procedures) are the easiest to develop.

Table S.1 provides our assessment of whether a given KSAO category should be the focus of development for future DoD diversity leaders. We note that, based on our analysis of job postings and interviews, applicants for senior diversity positions should have all of these KSAOs from the outset—i.e., they form the basis for selection.

Table S.1
Conclusions About Development Potential of KSAOs for Future Diversity Leaders

KSAO Category	Development Potential
KSAOs from Interviews	
Interpersonal skills	Evidence suggests that these can be improved through interventions. However, individuals with very poor interpersonal skills would not likely improve to the levels required for diversity leadership.
Business expertise	Technical aspects of business expertise, such as how to draft a policy document, can be provided via training. Business expertise based on deep knowledge of how the organization's core functions operate will likely require work experience to acquire.
Leadership skills	Technical aspects of leadership skills, such as identifying key organizational players to help promote diversity goals, can be developed over time through work experience. Leadership skills closely aligned with intrapersonal and interpersonal skills (e.g., knowing how to influence people) develop over time and may be less amenable to development.
EEO/MEO, AA, and diversity knowledge and skill	EEO/MEO, AA, and diversity topics can be learned through training, education, and on-the-job experience.
Personality and attitudes	Personality characteristics are among the most difficult KSAOs to modify. However, Cox and Beale (1997) suggest that diversity competence can be developed through learning processes.
Analytical abilities and skills	Analytical skills, such as data analysis, can be improved through training and education.
KSAOs Not Featured in Interviews	
Critical thinking and problem-solving	Critical thinking and problem-solving skills can be improved through training and education. However, these are complex skills that take time to develop. On-the-job experience with the types of problems faced in the area of D&I can be leveraged to assist future diversity leaders in enhancing their problem-solving skills.
Multicultural competence	Although training may increase awareness of diversity issues, developing multicultural competence is a learning process that takes time and requires some self-development.

DoD Should Determine Training and Education Requirements for Diversity Leader Positions

There Is No Consensus on Work, Training, and Education Experiences for Diversity Leaders, but Some Themes Emerge

Based on our content analysis of interview themes, we found no broad consensus among those we interviewed on what work history, training, or education diversity leaders must have. The lack of consensus was primarily the result of the lack of a professional track for diversity leaders, regardless of organizational setting, and the vast array of conferences, training events, and other diversity-related activities available to individuals seeking to learn more about D&I practices. Although we did not find broad consensus, we did note some recurring, more general themes. Both DoD and non-DoD interviewees cited the benefits of HR experience and business (operational) experience. DoD interviewees also noted personnel management experience as valuable.

With respect to education and training, DoD interviewees saw benefit in EEO compliance and legislation; unconscious bias; management, leadership, and organizational culture; human capital and personnel issues; language and culture; and analytical tools and statistics. Most of those we interviewed outside DoD had taken some training and education courses, but they also noted benefiting from conferences that dealt with diversity and leadership.

Both groups identified several courses, programs, and conferences that they either had attended, had sent staff to attend, or would recommend. Both groups also specifically cited Georgetown's and Cornell's diversity management programs, the Society for Human Resource Management, and Diversity Management and Equal Opportunity Institute courses. Those in DoD also referred to courses provided by military education institutions, such as the Joint Military Course at the National Defense University. Those in DoD who had come from industry brought up the Conference Board.

Given a lack of consensus on required training, we also reviewed nine diversity programs offered by civilian institutions. These programs offer courses in four topic areas: (1) equal opportunity (EO)/AA, (2) diversity, (3) HR, and (4) skills/practical applications. At least half of the programs offer an EO/AA legal course (Topic 1), diversity theory and history (Topic 2), change management/diversity initiatives (Topic 2), recruiting/staffing (Topic 3), and retention (Topic 3). The skill areas from Topic 4 match many of the other KSAOs identified by our interviewees as important for diversity leaders.

We Recommend Three Steps for Determining How to Train and Educate Future DoD Diversity Leaders

Because DoD typically develops its own leaders, it must identify how personnel can obtain required training and education to become diversity leaders. Although conducting the analysis to inform the following steps is beyond the scope of the current study, we recommend three steps for DoD's efforts to develop its future diversity leaders through education and training.

Step 1: Determine Whether There Should Be a Separate Professional Development Track for D&I Personnel. Before deciding how future D&I leaders should be trained and educated, DoD will first need to decide whether to establish a distinct professional development track for civilian and military personnel with D&I responsibilities or to create a developmental pathway for a larger group of personnel who perform D&I, EEO/MEO, and perhaps other HR-related activities. This step will help instill a sense of professional identity and is a prerequisite for determining the number of students and types of training, education, and experiences to provide at different stages of a person's professional development.

Step 2: Determine Training and Education Requirements. Once the decision about a professional development track has been made and professional track(s) defined, DoD should develop relevant training and education requirements. Development should focus on KSAOs that are malleable/developable, such as EEO/MEO knowledge. Of the KSAOs that are amenable to development, some are rather generic (e.g., interpersonal skills), and some are more specialized (e.g., EEO/MEO, AA, diversity knowledge and skills). This latter distinction can be important when selecting a training or education provider. In-house training and education may be more appropriate for the development of a highly specialized skill, whereas external providers with a record of providing quality instruction are usually better at imparting more general knowledge and skills (Galanaki, Bourantas, and Papalexandris, 2008).

In addition to decisions about skill type and type of provider, DoD must calculate how many personnel need to be trained and educated and what types of training and education experiences they need at each career stage. The final output of this step will be the number of personnel at different organizational levels who require generic and specialized training and education to prepare them for diversity leadership roles.

Step 3: Determine Means for Fulfilling Training and Education Requirements. Finally, DoD will need to decide the means for providing training and education for future diversity leaders. A major decision for DoD is whether to insource or outsource the training and education. Insourcing would require DoD to provide instruction, whereas outsourcing would involve non-DoD (external) providers, such as non-DoD governmental organizations, D&I experts from academia, and for-profit training vendors. Although there are many purported costs and benefits associated with insourcing and outsourcing, little empirical evidence is available to point to which factors are useful in making decisions about whether to outsource training. One study by Galanaki, Bourantas, and Papalexandris (2008) offers an exception. Galanaki, Bourantas, and Papalexandris tested decision models involving factors that affect perceived benefits of outsourcing, which, in turn, predicted the decision to outsource. Companies that have invested heavily in their in-house training capability, are larger in size, and see training as a source of competitive advantage are less likely to perceive benefits of outsourcing training. However, the availability of training in the external market increases the perceived benefits of outsourcing training. The existence of training in the external market was weighted more heavily in decisions to outsource than most of the other factors, except training as a source of competitive advantage when the skills are job-specific or organization-specific.

Other factors that DoD will need to consider when deciding how to offer training and education for future diversity leaders include the following:

- **course development:** use of existing courses, modification of existing courses, or development of new courses
- **time** requirements for courses
- **quality of instruction** (ideally measured by independent subject matter experts, such as accreditation organizations)
- **venue:** online, face to face at non-DoD locations (e.g., a brick-and-mortar academic institution), and/or face to face at DoD locations (e.g., DoD training locations, DoD work sites)
- **flexibility** in course modification (which will likely be lower when outsourcing)
- **development of an in-house training capability** (e.g., developing a train-the-trainer model in which outside experts train DoD instructors)
- **instilling new ideas** into the organization (perceived as more likely to come from outsourcing [Galanaki, Bourantas, and Papalexandris, 2008])
- **financial costs** (tuition/fees for outsourced training, travel and room and board for offsite locations, course development costs if new courses are developed, instructor costs for in-house training, etc.).

Unfortunately, none of these factors can be fit into a predetermined formula; rather, they must be weighed in accordance with priorities set by DoD decisionmakers. Moreover, uncertainty will be higher in decisions involving new courses or programs than those involving the use of existing courses and programs. Furthermore, DoD must infer the quality of potential courses either by reviewing courses that are similar to the ones desired or by evaluating the administrative and instructional reputation of the institutions or vendors willing to develop the new courses.

Acknowledgments

We wish to thank several people for their support of this project. We begin by thanking Clarence Johnson (principal director of ODMEO) for his sponsorship of the project. We also thank Beatrice Bernfeld, our current action officer, and Stephanie Miller, our former action officer, for their continued support throughout the project. Furthermore, we thank ODMEO staff for providing helpful feedback and, more generally, their expertise on diversity and inclusion. We also offer our gratitude to the Office of Personnel Management's Office of Diversity and Inclusion for providing insight into recent efforts to identify competencies for diversity professionals.

This project would not have been complete without the generosity of our study participants. We thank the 16 senior leaders and diversity and EEO/MEO directors in the service components and the National Guard Bureau who offered their insights on what they envision as the key roles and responsibilities for DoD diversity leaders. We also thank the 47 chief diversity officers and other diversity leaders from public and private organizations who spoke with us about their backgrounds and the work they do to promote diversity and inclusion.

Finally, we would be remiss if we did not thank our RAND colleagues for their support. John Winkler, Jennifer Lamping Lewis, and Nelson Lim offered their guidance throughout the project. Lynn Scott and Rosemary Hays-Thomas provided critical reviews of our work, which greatly improved its quality. Mollie Rudnick worked with another team member to code interviews. Shira Efron conducted literature searches, and Megan Clifford searched for diversity leaders outside

DoD for us to interview. Nolan Sweeney, Robert Stewart, and Abigail Haddad took excellent interview notes. Julie Ann Tajiri provided continuing administrative support.

Abbreviations

AA	affirmative action
CCDP/AP	Cornell Certified Diversity Professional/Advanced Practitioner
CDO	chief diversity officer
CDP	certification as a diversity professional
D&I	diversity and inclusion
DAC	developmental assessment center
DDWG	Defense Diversity Working Group
DEOMI	Defense Equal Opportunity Management Institute
DMP	diversity management program
DoD	U.S. Department of Defense
EO	equal opportunity
EEO	equal employment opportunity
HR	human resources
KSAOs	knowledge, skills, abilities, and other personal characteristics
MEO	military equal opportunity

NGB   National Guard Bureau

ODMEO   Office of Diversity Management and Equal
            Opportunity

OPM   Office of Personnel Management

SHRM   Society for Human Resource Management

SME   subject matter expert

CHAPTER ONE

Introduction

In August of 2011, the President of the United States issued Executive Order 13583, "Establishing a Coordinated Government-Wide Initiative to Promote Diversity and Inclusion in the Federal Workforce" (White House, 2011). In this Executive Order, the President directs "executive departments and agencies (agencies) to develop and implement a more comprehensive, integrated, and strategic focus on diversity and inclusion as a key component of their human resources strategies." As a first phase, the director of the Office of Personnel Management (OPM) and the deputy director for Management of the Office of Management and Budget were directed to coordinate with the President's Management Council and the chair of the Equal Employment Opportunity Commission in establishing a government-wide diversity and inclusion (D&I) initiative. OPM's Office of Diversity and Inclusion published the government-wide plan later in 2011.

The President's Executive Order also directed each executive department and agency to develop its own strategic plan for promoting a diverse workforce. In response to this directive, the U.S. Department of Defense (DoD) published its D&I strategic plan in 2012. This plan includes three main goals:

- Ensure leadership commitment to an accountable and sustained diversity effort.
- Employ an aligned strategic outreach effort to identify, attract, and recruit from a broad talent pool reflective of the nation DoD serves.
- Develop, mentor, and retain top talent from across the total force.

In addition to the DoD-wide plan, the services and the National Guard Bureau (DoD components) have built or are building their own D&I plans and, in so doing, employ individuals who are implementing or will implement D&I efforts. As these D&I plans evolve, DoD will have to determine what type of leadership roles are required for successful implementation of D&I plans and how those roles align with equal opportunity leadership roles. To that end, the Office of Diversity Management and Equal Opportunity (ODMEO) asked RAND to identify the key attributes and experiences needed by the individuals who will be primarily responsible for implementation of D&I plans in DoD. We refer to these individuals as *DoD diversity leaders* for simplicity, although they may be more accurately described as *diversity management leaders* or *D&I leaders*. In Table 1.1, we provide definitions of key terms we use throughout this report.

Study Questions and Approach

We designed our study to address the following three questions:

1. What are the key requirements for the position of a DoD diversity leader?
2. What attributes and experiences may be needed to perform those requirements?
3. What would DoD need to do to develop its future diversity leaders?

The questions are sequential, such that answers to the first question affect answers to the second and third questions. We designed the study to follow this sequencing by using a form of *job analysis*, which is a systematic process "directed toward discovering, understanding, and describing what people do at work" (Brannick et al., 2007, p. 1). Job analysis is oriented toward understanding work and/or worker attri-

Table 1.1
Definitions of Key Diversity-Related Terms

Key Term	Definition
Affirmative action (AA)	DoD defines *affirmative action* for military personnel as the "processes, activities, and systems designed to prevent, identify, and eliminate unlawful discriminatory treatment as it affects the recruitment, training, assignment, utilization, promotion, and retention of military personnel."[a]
Diversity and inclusion (D&I)	• DoD defines *diversity* as "all the different characteristics and attributes of the DoD's Total Force, which are consistent with our core values, integral to overall readiness and mission accomplishment, and reflective of the nation we serve."[b] • *Inclusion* is "the degree to which an employee perceives that he or she is an esteemed member of the work group through experiencing treatment that satisfies his or her needs for belongingness and uniqueness."[c] • An *inclusive organization* is one "in which the diversity of knowledge and perspectives that members of different groups bring to the organization has shaped its strategy, its work, its management and operating systems, and its core values and norms for success."[d]
Diversity management	How organizations drive or affect the impact of diversity on key organizational outcomes through plans, policies, and practices to leverage diversity in service of the mission[e]
[Civilian] Equal employment opportunity (EEO)	"The right of all covered persons to work and advance on the basis of merit, ability, and potential, free from social, personal, or institutional barriers of prejudice or discrimination based unlawfully on race, sex, color, national origin, age, religion, disability, reprisal, marital status, sexual orientation, status as a parent, political affiliation, or other prohibited non-merit factors as prohibited by . . ." law (e.g., Title VII of the Civil Rights Act of 1964, as amended) and Executive Order (e.g., Executive Order 11478, "Equal Employment Opportunity in the Federal Government")[f]
Military equal opportunity (MEO)	"The right of all military personnel to participate in and benefit from programs and activities for which they are qualified. These programs and activities shall be free from social, personal, or institutional barriers that prevent people from rising to the highest level of responsibility possible."[f]

Table 1.1—Continued

Key Term	Definition
Knowledge, skills, abilities, and other personal characteristics (KSAOs)	• *Knowledge* is "the existence in memory of a retrievable set of technical facts, concepts, language, and procedures directly relevant to job performance."[g] • *Skills* are "developed or training capacity to perform tasks"[g] and vary in specificity to the job and organization. Skills can be basic (applying to most jobs—e.g., writing), cross-functional (generic skills across a broad range of jobs—e.g., organizing and planning), or occupation-specific (e.g., operating specific types of machinery).[h] • *Ability* is a "relatively enduring capacity to acquire skills or knowledge, and to carry out tasks at an acceptable level of proficiency where tools, equipment and machinery are not major elements."[g] • *Other personal characteristics* include "job-relevant interests, preferences, temperament, and personality characteristics that indicate how well an employee is likely to perform on a routine, day-to-day basis or how an employee is likely to adjust to a job's working conditions."[g]

SOURCES: [a] DoD (DoDD 1350.2, 1995, p. 17). [b] DoD (2012, p. 3). [c] Shore et al. (2011, p. 1265). [d] Holvino, Ferdman, and Merrill-Sands (2004, p. 249). [e] Military Leadership Diversity Commission (2011, p. 4). [f] DoD (DoDD 1020.02, 2009, pp. 1–2). [g] Brannick, Levine, and Morgeson (2007, p. 62). [h] Sackett and Laczo (2003, p. 25).

butes aligned with requirements of jobs (e.g., job tasks).[1] Therefore, as the first step in our job analysis, we sought to identify and describe the position requirements—key roles and responsibilities—of diversity leader positions in DoD. However, because of the evolving nature of

---

[1]   A related approach to assessing work behavior is *competency modeling*, which aims to link worker attributes to an organization's strategic business goals. Although we use job analysis for our analytic approach, we did not adhere to a "traditional" job analysis. (For a discussion comparing traditional job analysis and competency modeling, see Sanchez and Levine [2009].) Specifically, we reviewed competency models from scientific and trade literatures. We also considered competencies listed in job postings for diversity leaders. Our interviews with diversity leaders include questions about organizations' strategic D&I plans. Our DoD diversity interviews involved questions about future roles and responsibilities (and associated KSAOs and training/education requirements) and ideal structures for diversity offices, given their components' strategic diversity goals. Taken together, our approach attempts to address two key limitations of traditional job analysis: its agnosticism toward strategic organizational goals and its focus on jobs as they are currently designed.

diversity leadership positions, we focused on future requirements for these positions in DoD. The second research task aligns with the second study question and was focused on identifying the KSAOs needed to meet those job demands. Finally, the third research task of the study involved linking results from the previous two tasks to provide recommendations regarding selection and development of key KSAOs necessary in DoD diversity leader positions.

In conducting our job analysis, we drew from different sources to provide a broader picture of the requirements of diversity leadership positions and those who fill those positions. We further designed our study tasks to place greater emphasis on specific sources to address the different study questions.

Information Sources for Study

Our primary source of information about DoD diversity leader position requirements comes from our interviews of DoD subject matter experts (SMEs) on diversity leadership and EEO/MEO leadership roles in DoD. Specifically, we interviewed 16 diversity leaders across the five military services[2] and the National Guard Bureau (NGB). Six of the 16 were senior-level leaders (general/flag officers or senior executive service civilians) with primary responsibility for diversity management in their components (akin to chief diversity officers [CDOs]) or with diversity and/or equal opportunity (EO) as part of a larger portfolio—e.g., manpower and personnel. We identified most of the senior leaders from their membership on the Defense Diversity Working Group (DDWG), which is primarily responsible for decisions regarding implementation of DoD's strategic D&I plan. The other ten leaders were directors or chiefs of diversity and/or EO programs in the services and NGB. Most of these leaders are at the O-5/O-6 military officer ranks or the GS-15 civilian-equivalent level. For simplicity, we refer to these ten individuals as "diversity and EEO/MEO directors" to differentiate them from the six senior DoD leaders we interviewed. Most of the ten diversity

---

[2]   Although the Coast Guard is part of the Department of Homeland Security, it has membership in DoD's diversity working groups. We therefore included Coast Guard leaders in our interviews.

and EEO/MEO directors are members of working groups that support the DDWG. Out of the 20 individuals we contacted for interviews, 16 granted interviews, for a response rate of 80 percent. The goal of the DoD interviews was to gather information on the key roles and responsibilities for *future* DoD diversity leadership positions focused on a director (or equivalent) level,[3] including how the roles and responsibilities might differ from those required to carry out EO efforts within DoD. We used a future-oriented approach for these interviews because of the evolving nature of the positions in DoD; because the positions were expected to change, asking about positions as they were at the time could miss important roles and responsibilities for future positions. To provide context for the future roles and responsibilities, we also asked about KSAOs associated with the roles and responsibilities and models for structuring diversity offices in DoD components.

Because of the small number of DoD SMEs on diversity and the changing nature of diversity leadership positions, we sought another source for information.[4] We therefore interviewed senior-level diversity leaders (e.g., CDOs) in organizations outside DoD. To identify individuals to interview, we conducted searches for companies with CDOs or senior diversity leaders using general search engines (e.g., Google), via websites for diversity or human resources (HR) professionals (e.g., shrm.org, diversityinc.org), and through consultation with our sponsor's office. To provide a representative sample of organization types, we drew our sample from the private sector (for-profit and not-for-

---

[3] We did not ask DoD study participants to identify the key roles and responsibilities of their current positions. Instead, we asked them what they envisioned would be the key roles and responsibilities for diversity (management) leader positions. We provided a definition of the position as one involving responsibility for implementing D&I policies, programs, and procedures in their components. This places the focus on the director (or equivalent) level, as opposed to senior-level leaders who oversee those responsible for implementing D&I policies, programs, and procedures.

[4] Although identification of KSAOs was the main purpose of conducting interviews with non-DoD diversity leaders, we also asked non-DoD interviewees to describe their key roles and responsibilities and their professional work, training, and educational experiences. As noted in Chapter Two, because of the limited scope of the DoD interviewee responses on roles and responsibilities, we later decided to integrate the findings from analysis of roles and responsibilities of non-DoD diversity leaders.

profit), higher education, federal government, and state or local government. Within those four categories, we then sampled organizations of various sizes (based on the number of employees), industries, and geographic locations within the United States. We identified 97 individuals to contact. However, 15 individuals had missing or incorrect contact information, resulting in 82 individuals to contact. In addition to these 82 individuals, we identified another 15 individuals through snowball methods (i.e., we asked interviewees for recommendations on whom to interview). Of the 97 individuals we contacted, 47 participated, for a 48-percent response rate.

We then supplemented our findings from the interviews with three additional sources of information:

- a review of empirical and trade literature on diversity leadership and leadership in general[5]
  - Our literature review focused on three content areas: (1) roles and responsibilities of senior diversity leaders such as CDOs, (2) KSAOs or competencies of senior diversity leaders and diversity professionals, and (3) training or other professional experiences and credentials acquired by senior diversity leaders or diversity professionals. For the second content area, KSAOs/competencies, we identified six models for diversity leader competencies. However, we also reviewed relevant literature on general management and leadership KSAOs/competencies to bolster our results.
- an analysis of roles and responsibilities and key KSAOs listed in online job postings for diversity leaders
  - From mid-December 2012 to early January 2013, we searched for diversity leader position opening descriptions ("job post-

---

[5] During the course of our study, the Society for Human Resource Management (SHRM) was in the process of setting voluntary standards for chief D&I officers (see Hays-Thomas and Bendick, 2013). However, we did not review the standards because they were not finished by the time our study was completed. At a panel discussion during the annual meeting for the Society for Industrial and Organizational Psychology on April 25, 2015, a SHRM representative, Debra Cohen, stated that SHRM's standards-setting process was currently on hold. We therefore cannot comment on when the standards will become available.

ings") on general employment websites (e.g., Monster.com) and employment websites for positions in higher education (e.g., Chronicle.com), human resource management (e.g., shrm.org), and federal government (e.g., GovernmentJobs.com). We identified thousands of hits, but most were redundant (i.e., they were for the same positions). After scanning description titles, we identified and analyzed 53 postings for diversity leader positions outside DoD.

- an examination of the program characteristics and content of a small sample of diversity education programs at higher-education institutions
  - We reviewed publicly available information on a small sample ($n = 9$) of diversity programs offered by six higher-education institutions. We chose a convenience sample to highlight well-known programs and only included programs that were active as of fall 2013. To be included, programs had to target individuals in the fields of diversity management and/or EEO and culminate in a degree or certificate.

We provide more detail on each of these sources and our methodology in Appendixes A, B, and C.

Analytic Approach for Interviews and Job Postings

As described in Appendixes A and B, we used content coding methodology to analyze job postings and interviews. Our analytic approach was developed for job postings and then adapted for the interviews. We used an iterative process to develop the coding scheme and analyze the job posting content. First, two team members who were experts in job analytic methods open-coded job posting content to identify relevant themes. The themes formed the basis of the codes, which were grouped into categories to develop a coding scheme. Using QSR NVivo 9 software, a third team member with expertise in content coding methodology coded the job postings. The two job-analysis experts independently reviewed the coding results and met with each other and the third team member to identify and resolve disagreements.

Because the interviews provide richer data than job postings do, we expanded the coding scheme for the interviews. Throughout this report, we use the term *CDO codebook* to refer to the coding scheme for the interviews. We used a similar coding approach for the interviews as we did for the job postings. The main exception is that two individuals conducted the coding of non-DoD interview content because of the volume of information provided by those interviews. The two coders began by coding the same interviews together and then coded the same set independently to determine interrater agreement. An iterative process was used to achieve a high level of agreement between coders. The two job-analysis experts then reviewed the results and integrated the findings with those from other sources to identify themes.

In this report, we discuss our main findings in an integrative fashion, although we analyzed the DoD interviews, non-DoD interviews, and job postings separately. We used an integrative approach because diversity leadership positions are relatively new in organizations, particularly in DoD. We expected variability in how experts described diversity leadership roles, responsibilities, and KSAOs. We therefore culled information from different sources to capture this variability. We also used different sources to compensate for shortcomings of any single source. For example, as we discuss in Chapter Two, our DoD interviewees did not provide as much description of roles and responsibilities for *future* DoD diversity leader roles as we anticipated. We therefore used information from the other interviews and job postings to fill in the gaps left by DoD interviewees. The main limitation with our approach is that the job postings and non-DoD interviews reflect existing position requirements, not future position requirements. To address this limitation, we reviewed literature on leadership and diversity leadership, as well as diversity education programs. The literature and diversity education programs provide insights into what D&I and leadership experts consider important KSAOs for diversity leadership positions, as well as the role of training and education in developing KSAOs for diversity leaders.

Although we integrate findings across sources to identify themes, we conducted two additional analyses to identify relevant differences between groups within each interview sample. We focused on the roles and responsibility categories and the KSAOs outlined in the body of the report. First, we compared non-DoD participants by organization type—for-profit and not-for-profit. We examined organization type because we expected that the responsibilities of for-profit (corporate) diversity leaders could differ somewhat from those of not-for-profit diversity leaders. Moreover, experiences of not-for-profit diversity leaders outside DoD should more closely relate to experiences of DoD diversity leaders because DoD is a not-for-profit institution.[6] Second, we compared the six senior-level DoD leaders to the ten DoD diversity and EEO/MEO leaders. For both sets of analyses, we conducted Fisher's exact test to test a null hypothesis of no association between group membership and endorsement of each role/responsibility category and KSAO category described in the main body of the report. We chose this test because of the small sample sizes.[7] If we did not find a significant result at a probability of 0.05, we did not discuss the results of the secondary analyses at length.

Limitations of Our Approach

No study is without limitations, and our study is no exception. Although we use multiple sources to address our three study questions, we primarily rely on the expertise of those we interviewed. Importantly, we did not empirically validate the KSAOs against diversity leaders' performance or other important organizational outcomes. The D&I field as a whole faces this limitation because an agreed-upon set of KSAOs has not been identified. However, we believe our study's strength comes from the multiple perspectives offered by our different sources and the tailoring of the training and education discussion to the needs of DoD.

---

[6]   We also considered comparing interviews with EEO/AA/civil rights responsibilities and those without such responsibilities. However, the relationship between organization type and EEO/AA/civil rights responsibilities suggested that results would be similar for both types of comparisons. Specifically, 65 percent of not-for-profit interviewees have EEO/AA/civil rights responsibilities versus only 24 percent of corporate diversity leaders.

[7]   See Agresti (1996) for a discussion of Fisher's exact test.

Organization of This Report

The remaining chapters of this report describe the findings and recommendations from our analysis of the KSAOs needed by diversity leaders. Chapter Two describes findings regarding the roles and responsibilities for diversity leaders. Chapter Three outlines our findings about the KSAOs diversity leaders might need to fill those roles and responsibilities successfully. In that chapter, we focus primarily on the findings from the non-DoD leader interviews but supplement those results with information from our DoD interviews, the literature on diversity leadership competencies, and job postings for diversity leader positions. Chapter Four describes the selection and development of KSAOs for diversity leaders. The chapter describes the malleability of leadership KSAOs; the professional development of diversity leaders through prior work, training, and educational experiences; and educational content from our review of diversity education programs at higher-education institutions. Finally, Chapter Five brings together the findings from Chapters Two through Four by providing conclusions regarding key KSAOs necessary for diversity leader positions in DoD and offering a three-step plan for developing future diversity leaders in DoD.

CHAPTER TWO

Roles and Responsibilities for Diversity Leaders

The first step of a job analysis and determining the key KSAOs needed is to define the job demands—in this case, the primary roles and responsibilities of diversity leader positions. We interviewed a wide range of people with responsibilities for diversity in both industry and in DoD. All told, we spoke with 61 people with diversity (and/or EEO/MEO) leadership roles.[1] Additionally, we supplemented our interviews by analyzing the roles and responsibilities described in a sample of online job postings for diversity leaders.

Overall, the role and responsibility categories identified by diversity leaders in the two groups and across job postings overlap substantially. The degree of overlap is notable for two reasons. First, the frame of reference for roles and responsibilities differed between the two types of interviews: Non-DoD leaders were asked to describe their current roles and responsibilities, whereas DoD leaders were asked to describe what they envisioned for the roles and responsibilities of a DoD diversity leader in general. Second, our non-DoD leader sample and the job postings represent leaders from a variety of organizations across industries.

Within DoD, we note that some variation occurs between organizations. Although the services and NGB have diversity leader positions, they can vary in their specific demands. For example, some DoD

---

[1]   We spoke with 47 non-DoD personnel and 16 from DoD. However, because two of the people from the non-DoD group did not hold senior diversity leadership positions, we removed their responses from analyses directly tied to senior diversity leadership positions, such as roles and responsibilities (non-DoD role/responsibility $n = 45$).

diversity leaders may have EO and D&I responsibilities, whereas other leaders are responsible for D&I alone. Given these possible demand differences, we spoke with DoD diversity and EEO/MEO leaders to ask what they envisioned as the roles and responsibilities of DoD diversity leaders (and how those compared with DoD EEO/MEO leaders).[2] We also asked them to describe their ideal model for a diversity office, including what the main staff responsibilities would be and the civilian-military mix of staff, whether the diversity leader should be civilian or military, and what the reporting chain should look like. We asked about office structure because how a diversity office is structured and positioned in an organization can affect the roles and responsibilities of a diversity leader.

In the sections below, we describe our findings regarding the primary roles and responsibilities for diversity leaders. We begin with a discussion of themes identified in our interviews and our analysis of online job postings for diversity leader positions. We conclude with a description of themes regarding DoD diversity office structure and the impact that structure may have on diversity leader roles and responsibilities within DoD.

Views on Roles and Responsibilities for Diversity Leaders

Based on our interviews and analysis of job postings, we identified four main overarching categories of roles and responsibilities: strategic leadership, stakeholder engagement, tracking diversity trends, and HR-related activities. Table 2.1 presents a description of each of these categories, as well as the percentage of interview participants who mentioned each type. It is important to note, however, that interviewees were responding to open-ended questions. Therefore, participants may have neglected to mention important areas, which would affect the

---

[2] Many stakeholders responded to this question by discussing the KSAOs needed for diversity leaders, rather than the job responsibilities for that type of position. Others answered the question by describing current roles and responsibilities, as opposed to what they believed those should be in an ideal situation. These examples are not drawn from stakeholder descriptions of their own backgrounds and current roles and responsibilities.

Table 2.1
Roles and Responsibilities for Diversity Leaders Identified by Interviewees

Role/ Responsibility	Description	% of Participants Identifying This Role	
		DoD (*n* = 16)	Non-DoD (*n* = 45)
Strategic leadership	Creating and/or implementing a strategic vision for D&I. Engages in strategic planning, develops policies and programs/initiatives, and provides consultation to senior leadership on policies.	56	100
Stakeholder engagement	Educating internal stakeholders about diversity initiatives and general diversity-related issues, as well as representing the organization to the community and engaging with external stakeholders. Involves promoting a diverse, inclusive, and respectful work environment.	81	100
Tracking diversity trends	Includes monitoring internal diversity and EEO metrics, as well as external diversity trends and best practices	25	84
HR-related activities	Develops and may help to implement strategies to recruit, select, and retain diverse talent	19	73

NOTES: Categories are listed in order of descending frequency. To the extent possible, these descriptions match those used in the CDO codebook.

percentages. Moreover, percentages can change dramatically with a change of one person for the small DoD sample (e.g., moving from four to five people would change the percentage from 25 to 31 percent). Because of the small DoD sample, we caution against comparing the exact values of the percentages for the DoD and non-DoD samples.

Although not presented in the table, our analysis of the job postings revealed similar categories of roles and responsibilities as interviews.[3] In the sections below, we describe each of these categories of roles and responsibilities in more detail. Where they are apparent, we

---

[3] To conserve space, we do not cite detailed job posting results here; the detailed results are in Appendix B.

also comment on the differences between the responses of DoD and non-DoD participants, as well as differences among responses across DoD components and between senior leaders and the diversity and EEO/MEO directors who work under the senior leaders. In particular, we analyzed differences based on the following:

- for-profit (n = 25) versus not-for-profit (n = 20) non-DoD participants
- senior-level DoD leaders (n = 6) versus DoD diversity and EEO/MEO leaders (n = 10).

We note where groups differed significantly using a probability value of 0.05 on Fisher's exact test. Interestingly, only one relationship came out significant: DoD interviewee perceptions as to whether the EEO/MEO function should be separate from the diversity function. We discuss these differences later in this chapter in the section titled "Diversity Compared with EEO/MEO in DoD."

In the following sections, we discuss each of the role/responsibility categories. Within those categories are subcategories. Percentages for the non-DoD sample subcategories are available in Table B.30 in Appendix B. We do not include the subcategory percentages for the DoD sample in the appendix because of concerns of identification by inference with small sample sizes. However, where percentages were reasonably sized (25 percent or higher), we include them in our discussion.

Strategic Leadership

All of the non-DoD interviewees and over half of the DoD interviewees identified responsibilities related to strategic leadership, and this theme was present in interviews with all but one DoD component. A key aspect of strategic leadership is creating and/or implementing a strategic vision for D&I. This includes engaging in strategic planning, developing policies and diversity programs and initiatives, and providing consultation to senior leadership on policies.

Overall, 87 percent of non-DoD diversity leaders identified creating and implementing a strategic D&I vision and strategy for the organization as being a key responsibility under strategic leadership. One corporate interviewee stated:

> I am accountable for informing and advocating for policies and a diversity strategy that aligns with our overall mission and business strategy to help us achieve business outcomes.

Interestingly, only two senior DoD leaders identified responsibilities related to strategic leadership. The rest of those comments came from the DoD diversity and EEO/MEO directors we interviewed. It is possible that senior DoD leaders see their roles as involving strategic leadership and do not think of the roles of diversity and EEO/MEO directors as strategic. However, as noted by seven of the ten diversity and EEO/MEO directors, leaders at their level engage in strategic leadership activities, as described below.

The interviewees who identified strategic leadership as an important responsibility noted that D&I should be mission-driven rather than focused on EEO/MEO-related compliance. It follows that diversity leaders should be involved in developing the strategy to support that mission. As one non-DoD interviewee explains:

> My general responsibility is setting the diversity mission, vision, and strategy. I work on a global level to institute the tactics that are associated with that vision. That would include three major areas of focus: how are we managing, not talent recruiting, but employee engagement; brand and reputation; and business impact.

At least in the case of DoD, diversity leaders also draft policies and procedures to execute the organization's diversity strategy. Drafting policy is often accompanied by a need to advise senior leaders in those areas. Multiple stakeholders emphasized the importance of that advisory role, which was also discussed under the umbrella of stakeholder engagement. One DoD interviewee described the diversity leader's role as follows:

Create policy and provide recommendations to senior leaders that accompany diversity, demographic, all kinds of diversity . . . and how it impacts operations, policy, etc.

About 82 percent of non-DoD diversity leaders and about a third of DoD diversity leaders also noted responsibilities for diversity initiatives and programs in their organizations as part of their strategic leadership responsibility. They provide oversight of diversity programs, such as those involving employee resource groups, diversity leadership councils or forums, and internal organization events (e.g., diversity awards day). They also coordinate with other senior leaders in the organization to promote these programs, but their staffs run the day-to-day operations of the programs (e.g., coordinating schedules for affinity group meetings). Additionally, some individuals noted that while diversity leaders may not be directly responsible for individual diversity programs, they may be involved in evaluating them. For example, one DoD interviewee described how his or her current role relates to diversity programs, stating:

Because I don't own any specific programs. My role is to— facilitate, integrate, collaborate. Monitor and assess. Drive policy.

Although diversity leaders may not be directly involved in implementing programs and training, interviewees did suggest that those responsibilities belong to the diversity office as a whole. Thus, it follows that leaders must promote and support individual diversity programs and initiatives.

Two other less-frequently mentioned strategic leadership responsibilities shared by some non-DoD diversity leaders include promoting a culture that values D&I (42 percent) and strategic messaging and marketing (38 percent). For some non-DoD diversity leaders, promoting a diverse and inclusive culture is their main responsibility:

My primary responsibility is to ensure that the workplace is maintained in a manner so that individuals believe that we have a climate of fairness, inclusion, and is free from harassment, where every employee can reach their potential and have a positive impact on our mission.

Strategic messaging and marketing involves such activities as providing oversight of how diversity is portrayed on the organization's website and on social media accounts and presenting to employee or leadership groups on D&I initiatives. Strategic messaging and marketing allows diversity leaders to communicate the diversity vision, mission, and initiatives within and outside the organization.

Stakeholder Engagement

Eighty-one percent of DoD interviewees and 100 percent of non-DoD interviewees identified responsibilities related to stakeholder engagement, including at least one interviewee from each DoD component. This overarching category involves advising senior leaders on diversity issues and strategies, educating internal stakeholders on diversity, and engaging external stakeholders on diversity.

Many (63 percent) of our DoD interviewees and 96 percent of our non-DoD interviewees specifically noted the importance of advising senior leaders to achieve D&I goals. However, for DoD diversity leaders, the path to senior leadership is not direct. As one DoD respondent stated:

> If you have a message you have to get it through all those wickets. It's about being able to influence your senior leaders. They don't see the face of diversity. It's buried four levels down. I have to have the same playing field to move forward to it.

In contrast with DoD diversity leaders, most of the non-DoD interviewees stated that they directly advise organizations' presidents, chief executive officers, and boards of directors. As one non-DoD interviewee explained:

> I'm [the university's] visible leader in terms of advising senior leadership on policies/programs/practices around diversity and multiculturalism, around how do you create excellence around

diversity at your university, best practices. I also advise the president on that and support other senior leaders on that.

The difference between DoD and non-DoD participants' access to top organizational leadership may be a function of the strong hierarchical structure of DoD. Corporate structures can be flatter, allowing a CDO in a corporation direct access to the chief executive officer and other top leaders.

In addition to advising senior leaders, diversity leaders—particularly non-DoD diversity leaders—identified internal engagement with the rest of the organization as a key responsibility. For example, one non-DoD interviewee stated:

> Big picture—my job is to ensure that our organization is highly aware of all of our diversity and inclusion efforts throughout the business. Providing articles, or information for our online intranet. Might mean providing presentations for employee meetings. . . . The training or learning can come in a variety of formats—might be formal classroom-type training, might be educational offerings that employee resource groups provide to the organizations, might be external engagement—either me presenting out what we're doing or learning externally and then coming back and sharing about benchmarking trends, that kind of thing.

Although a few DoD interviewees mentioned training on diversity issues, DoD interviewees tended to focus more on engaging external stakeholders on diversity issues. External engagement was also the most-mentioned form of stakeholder engagement in the job postings we analyzed. External engagement takes on different flavors across industries. For DoD, much external engagement is focused on recruiting talent to join the military. As one DoD interviewee put it:

> Messaging is big. We spend. . . . I know the O-6 is out on the road, maybe going to HACU [Hispanic Association of Colleges and Universities], going to things. Messaging. You're the individual who goes to external organizations, get them to understand how we're recruiting. . . . Even though we [the service overall] do

have recruiters, some of us [the diversity personnel] also usually show up to be on panel, talk to organizations. External communications [are] important.

Many corporate diversity leaders discussed external engagement in the context of both recruiting talent and branding (to increase market share and expand into other markets). Another form of external engagement in the corporate sector focuses on customer and supplier diversity (i.e., increasing the diversity of firms that the organization serves [customers] or of firms that provide goods and services to the organization [suppliers]). One interviewee in the private sector describes how the organization provides diversity guidance to other companies that are customers:

> A lot of companies are our customers. . . . A lot are much further behind on diversity. As a value-add to them, we consult with them. We give them our strategies, we show them our different programs, initiatives, education programs to help them build their own.

Tracking Diversity Trends

Among DoD personnel, only four individuals—or 25 percent—across three components identified responsibilities related to tracking diversity trends. However, many more non-DoD interviewees (84 percent)[4] discussed responsibilities involved with tracking diversity trends. The low endorsement level for DoD participants may be partly a function of the methodology we used (open-ended questions) and partly a function of the substantive organizational differences between DoD and organizations represented in our non-DoD sample. For example, unlike other federal government entities, DoD employs military and civilian personnel, is much larger in size, and includes components (e.g., the services) that have different cultures. Monitoring diversity trends may

---

[4]   Differences between corporate and not-for-profit interviewees were not significant (88 percent versus 80 percent, respectively).

be particularly challenging for DoD because of its size, different service cultures, and different categories of personnel.

The majority of non-DoD interviewees (73 percent) focused on the importance of tracking internal organizational trends related to diversity. Tracking internal diversity trends includes developing and using workforce representation metrics to meet organizational goals. For example, one non-DoD interviewee stated:

> We also compile and report how we're progressing on the workforce. It's my group that sets goals for the divisions and senior leaders at the company. . . . Each division CEO's bonus is tied to meeting those diversity performance goals. There's a quantitative measure of that that's purely representation—same for everyone—and a number of measurable goals that aren't directly related to workforce numbers but that include things from a workforce/workplace perspective and the marketplace.

Tracking internal trends may also involve employee surveys and tracking EEO complaints, as explained by one non-DoD diversity leader:

> I do analytics work also—my team does analysis in terms of employee survey feedback, trends to look at. Looking at trends in EO complaints.

Over a third (36 percent) of non-DoD interviewees mentioned tracking external diversity trends, which involves benchmarking and identifying best practices. Regardless of industry, senior diversity leaders benchmark the external labor market to help their organizations prepare for changes in recruiting talent. As one non-DoD interviewee explains:

> What will the workforce look like 10–15 years from now? So we're building for the future, when the workplace will look different. So [one of the goals is] getting executives to understand this from a talent perspective.

We can only speculate as to why participants mentioned tracking internal trends more often than tracking external trends. One possibility is access to information: It is much easier to collect and analyze information within one's own organization than to identify appropriate data from external sources. In particular, organizations may be concerned about sharing their workforce data with competitors and, therefore, do not release the information to outside entities unless required by law. Without appropriate data for benchmarking, external tracking becomes difficult, if not impossible.

Whether they are tracking internal or external diversity trends, many non-DoD diversity leaders have members of their staff who run the numbers and contribute to reports for senior leadership and the organization as a whole. The diversity leader's role is to relay the trends to leaders and the organization.

HR-Related Activities

When it came to HR-related activities, the divide between DoD and non-DoD representatives was, again, relatively sharp. Only three DoD individuals, each from a different DoD component and representing both senior-level (one person) and non–senior-level (two people) EEO/MEO and diversity positions, identified HR-related activities as an area in which a diversity leader would have responsibilities. Although we did not explicitly ask interviewees to discuss HR responsibilities, their omission suggests that DoD diversity leaders do not see these activities as central to a DoD diversity leader's role. Moreover, the interviewees who discussed HR-related activities stated that these activities should not be among a diversity management leader's primary responsibilities. However, they described ways in which a leader may be involved in HR-related activities. For example, one DoD respondent noted that diversity leaders may play a role in recruitment and outreach, stating:

> Even though we [the service overall] do have recruiters, some of us [the diversity personnel] also usually show up to be on panel, talk to organizations. External communications [are] important.

While HR-related tasks may not have been identified by DoD respondents as a key job responsibility, maintaining knowledge and awareness of activities in this area was seen as important.

In contrast, 73 percent of non-DoD interviewees mentioned HR-related activities as one of their important responsibilities.[5] In general, non-DoD interviewees do not have primary responsibility over HR activities but instead work with HR leadership to ensure that the organization is attracting, selecting, and retaining diverse talent. For example, one non-DoD interviewee stated:

> Part of what I do is work with the office of human resources to develop diverse hires. I help formulate interview questions. I am a voice around that table to remind HR about the importance of diversity, to ensure the process is fair and objective. I am also in charge of making sure that we're rating people in a way that is standardized and consistent.

In addition to the above categories of roles and responsibilities, about a third (38 percent) of our non-DoD interviewees mentioned general management responsibilities, such as evaluating staff and managing budgets.[6] Although not explicitly mentioned by our DoD participants, as we will discuss later, there are expectations that a diversity leader would manage an office with multiple staff and programs to oversee.

Notably, only 29 percent of our non-DoD interviewees listed EEO compliance and complaints management as one of their responsibilities.[7] We discuss the DoD perspective on the role of EEO/MEO in more detail below.

---

[5]   In our non-DoD sample, corporate diversity leaders cited HR-related activities at a higher percentage (84 percent) than not-for-profit diversity leaders (65 percent). However, our Fisher's exact test results indicate a nonsignificant difference between these two percentages.

[6]   Although a higher percentage of not-for-profit diversity leaders (50 percent) than corporate diversity leaders (28 percent) noted general management responsibilities, the difference did not come out significant in our test.

[7]   Again, a seemingly large difference in percentages between corporate diversity leaders (24 percent) and not-for-profit diversity leaders (45 percent) for EEO activities came out nonsignificant in testing.

Diversity Compared with EEO/MEO in DoD

Given that there are currently specific EO positions across DoD, we asked DoD interviewees if the roles and responsibilities they described for diversity leaders differed from what they would envision for an EEO/MEO leader. Of the 13 individuals who expressed an opinion, over 60 percent thought that the responsibilities should be separate. Disproportionate support for this position came from the diversity and EEO/MEO directors, who represented 75 percent of those who endorsed the idea of separate diversity and EEO/MEO functions. Senior leaders, on the other hand, were more likely to hold the opposite view. Two-thirds of the senior leaders interviewed said that they would not separate the diversity and EEO/MEO roles.

Responses also varied by component. Individuals' views may be influenced by the current EEO/MEO or diversity office arrangement in their organization. Some interviewees supported the current arrangement in their component; others would prefer to change it. One DoD individual noted that it would be difficult to change the existing structure in his or her organization:

> Those programs in and of themselves are so entrenched and have their own bureaucracies that you can't divorce them.

This individual commented that the arrangement—whether the two positions or offices could be separate or independent—may depend on the resources available to each component.

Interviewees noted that, whether or not the positions are combined, diversity leaders should have some knowledge of EEO/MEO policies; however, they should not be primarily responsible for compliance tasks. As previously discussed, most respondents believe that the responsibilities of diversity leaders are related to accomplishing a larger mission and are not limited to complying with EEO laws. One DoD individual drew that distinction as follows:

> Big difference between MEO and EEO—by law focuses on protected categories. Diversity is much broader in scope and not concerned so much about law, but mission performance and what

unique aspects will help mission performance. They overlap in many ways, but are distinct.

Where EEO/MEO leaders may identify indicators and trends, diversity leaders respond and take action, with a focus on promoting inclusion. However, senior leaders agreed that one individual could be responsible for both diversity and EEO/MEO tasks, with one DoD interviewee stating:

> I think it would be beneficial to have it together, because EEO is the foundation for diversity and inclusion, and if you have a strong EEO presence in the organization, you can do more.

Proposals for Structuring a Diversity Office in DoD

An area of particular interest for those in DoD is what a diversity office there might look like. This is also important to understand, given that how a diversity office is structured and positioned in an organization affects the roles and responsibilities, and the effectiveness, of a diversity leader. Therefore, in addition to asking about roles and responsibilities, we asked DoD interviewees to describe how they might structure a diversity management office in their component and how that office would relate to EEO/MEO and HR departments. DoD interviewees also commented on their desired staff roles and personnel mix and on where that office should be situated in the larger reporting chain in their component.

Division Between Diversity and EEO/MEO

The majority of respondents concurred that a diversity office should be distinct from an EO office, though support for this division was stronger in some components than others.[8] Many did note that the

---

[8] It should be noted that some of these responses came from the question about roles and responsibilities of diversity versus EEO/MEO leaders, and a few interviewees seemed to support their component's current arrangement by default.

offices should communicate and collaborate, but that a diversity office should not be occupied with EEO/MEO compliance issues. As one DoD interviewee stated:

> They have to be—it's like an airplane—they need to be connected, but EEO/MEO need to be separate and have their own function, or given their own lane to operate in. There needs to be regular communication, but different offices and different functions.

A few suggested that EEO/MEO and diversity could fall under one office, but these were in the minority. One interviewee suggested that the structure and division of offices may depend on the size of the component and resources available. We observed little variation between the opinions of senior leaders and diversity and EEO/MEO directors.

Few individuals commented on the relationship between diversity and HR offices. One respondent argued that diversity is part of talent management and therefore should fall under the HR office. This would facilitate efforts to maintain a diverse workforce. On the other hand, one individual insisted that the diversity office would be paralyzed if it fell under HR. We also heard that military and civilian HR offices should be partners. Opinions on whether they should fall under one office may vary across the components.

Personnel Mix

When asked about staffing a diversity office, respondents identified many types of experience that would be useful for staff members and also many roles that the diversity office could play. These included individuals trained in and responsible for the following:

- public affairs
- community outreach
- education and training
- budget and resource management
- measurement and analytics
- recruitment and talent management
- strategic planning

- administrative assistants
- development
- social responsibility.[9]

In addition, we heard that having a resident military expert and diversity specialist, and possibly an attorney, would be useful. The diversity office would also benefit from having dedicated regional liaisons to work in the field and represent different installations. One DoD individual emphasized the point that the work a diversity office needs to accomplish is too much for one leader:

> One person won't be able to do this by themselves. Need a cadre of SMEs who have the ability to strategize, who can create the analytical story. And who are able to strategically communicate what that story should be.

Another individual in DoD described the desired number of staff members:

> If I was going to design one now, I would have two administrative assistants, a director who would be a GS-15 or colonel, a deputy director who would be a GS-15 or -14, and then at least three others around the GS-13 level who would help answer any related taskers or requests. The administrative assistants could be an E-7 and then a civilian GS-7.

The majority of respondents believe that diversity offices should have both military and civilian personnel. However, whether the leader of a diversity office should be military or civilian was less clear. Respondents noted that while military leaders have credibility within their component, civilian leaders can provide stability. For example, one DoD interviewee commented that the benefit of having civilians is that they have experience and often stay in the office for a long time:

---

[9]   This list represents the range in responses we observed and presents a number of staff roles that should be considered. However, given the limited number of responses, we are not able to draw conclusions on the relative importance of each area.

Maybe the job needs to be civilianized—a GS-15 so there's some consistency, so as military come and go the message doesn't change.

On the other hand, military personnel have the advantage of credibility with service members. As one DoD individual commented:

Civilians bring long-term experience and as they stay for years, they understand the programs. That's great. But military— credibility with uniformed individuals. . . . They both have benefits.

Others also said that a diversity office would benefit from the inclusion of active duty, guard, and reserve staff, and that contractors may also be included.

Reporting Chain

Half of the DoD interviewees explicitly mentioned that it is important for diversity leaders to report directly to top leaders. They noted that the direct line of communication is essential for the diversity office and leader to be effective. A minority felt that the diversity leader should not report directly to top leaders. One DoD respondent summarized the benefit of having the position report to top leaders and the problems that could arise if that reporting chain is not in place:

First, the diversity management leader needs to report directly to the leader of the organization. As long as you have people who can be barriers to real-time communication, it will be a problem. You need to be in the room when policies, mission, directives are discussed. It has to be viewed as strategic, not operational or tactical.

Others echoed the concern about communication. If diversity leaders do not work directly for the top leaders of their component, then they may be "buried under processes and bureaucracy." Having that direct line could elevate the mission of the diversity office and enable diversity experts to educate top leaders. Another DoD individual noted that corporate diversity leaders directly report to top leaders and that arrangement should serve as a model for DoD:

> In the private sector, the CDO sits at a high level and reports to the top; they also have a budget and resources, their own office, integral part of the organization, measure ROI [return on investment], aligned to internal and external diversity (e.g., supplier diversity), and do diversity relations on a regular basis. . . . If there are no resources, staffing, and it's not high enough to influence strategy, DoD will not see a return on investment.

It is difficult to say whether support for a direct reporting arrangement varies across components or by leadership level because many respondents did not comment on this topic.

Summary

Diversity leaders perform many roles and responsibilities to develop and implement D&I strategies for their organizations. Diversity leaders perform strategic leadership functions, such as developing and promulgating a vision and strategy for D&I in the organization. Whether in DoD or elsewhere, diversity leaders also engage internal and external stakeholders, with a particular focus on advising senior leadership. They track internal and external diversity trends and work with (or within) HR to identify ways to promote a diversity focus in recruiting, hiring, and development practices. Some of these diversity leaders also "own" EEO or HR functions, requiring additional duties tied to EEO compliance and talent management. In particular, not-for-profit diversity leaders outside DoD may have more EEO functions to manage, whereas corporate diversity leaders may have more HR functions.

Having the right staff and office structure can help diversity leaders execute their primary roles and responsibilities. However, the DoD leaders we interviewed did not prescribe any model structure for DoD diversity offices. That said, many agreed that diversity and EEO/MEO leader responsibilities should be separate and that diversity offices should not be one-person shops. They cited a variety of experiences and roles for diversity office staff. Although there was no consensus on whether the diversity leaders should be military or civilian, they agreed that a mix of military and civilian personnel in the office would be ideal. Finally, about half felt that diversity leaders should have direct access to top leaders in the component. Thus, diversity leaders in DoD will also be responsible for general management and leadership functions in their roles and leading an office with multiple staff, as well as communicating with top leaders.

CHAPTER THREE
KSAOs for Diversity Leaders

To execute their roles and responsibilities successfully, diversity leaders need a host of KSAOs. In this chapter, we describe key KSAOs for diversity leaders based primarily on those noted by our interviewees. As in the previous chapter, we discuss places where findings differ among non-DoD diversity leaders based on organization type and EEO responsibility and whether DoD interview findings change when senior-level leader responses are removed. We supplement our discussion of the interview findings with those from our analysis of the job postings. We also offer comparisons to competency models for diversity leaders and KSAOs from research literature on leadership. Throughout the chapter, we interweave our findings from the job postings analysis and the literature with our main findings from the interviews.

KSAOs Identified by Diversity Leaders

We asked interviewees to describe the KSAOs necessary for fulfilling the responsibilities of a diversity leader that they identified in Chapter Two. Table 3.1 displays the main KSAOs identified by at least a quarter of non-DoD interviewees, as well as the percentage of DoD and non-DoD interview participants who mentioned each KSAO.[1] Again, it is

---

[1]   Although many additional KSAO categories were defined in the CDO codebook, only those apparent in both the DoD and non-DoD interviews are included here. Descriptions of the KSAOs within each KSAO category can be found in Table B.11 (and are repeated in Table B.31) in Appendix B.

Table 3.1
KSAOs for Diversity Leaders as Identified by Interviewees

KSAO Category	KSAO Subcategories	% of Participants Identifying This KSAO Category	
		DoD (*n* = 16)	Non-DoD (*n* = 47)
Interpersonal skills	• Communication • Influence/persuasion • Collaboration/teamwork • Intercultural interactions • Political savvy	88	94
Business expertise	• Intraorganizational expertise • HR knowledge and experience	<25	85
Leadership skills	• Strategic leadership skills and expertise • General management/leadership skills • Organizational improvement/change	63	77
EEO/MEO, AA, and diversity knowledge and skills	• Compliance and legislation • Knowledge of D&I	81	66
Personality and attitude	• Driven/motivated • Committed to diversity	25	64
Analytical abilities and skills	• Skills involving data and metrics	38	36

important to note that interviewees were responding to open-ended questions, so the percentage of interviewees who mentioned a specific KSAO should not necessarily be taken as an indication of relative importance, particularly across the two interview samples. Moreover, changes to the small DoD sample can greatly affect the percentages. However, some differences are discernable between DoD and non-DoD interviewees. For example, personality and attitude received more mentions than analytical abilities and skills in the non-DoD interview group, but the reverse holds for the DoD interview group. As another example, business expertise was mentioned by 85 percent of non-DoD interviewees but by less than 25 percent (i.e., fewer than four people) of DoD interviewees. Therefore, where possible, we note differences between the DoD and non-DoD samples in terms of main KSAO categories (e.g., interpersonal skills) and KSAO subcategories (e.g., communication).

We also noted some difference in emphases when analyzing job postings. The job postings listed more technical skill requirements (e.g., computer skills) than interviewees described. Job postings tend to ask for basic skill requirements that senior diversity leaders may not describe in interviews because they are assumed to have them already.

As in the previous chapter, we conducted secondary analyses to determine whether organization type in the non-DoD sample and leadership level in the DoD sample explain any differences within the two main samples. Specifically, we compared percentages for the main KSAO categories for the following groups:

- for-profit (n = 26) versus not-for-profit (n = 21) non-DoD participants
- senior-level DoD leaders (n = 6) versus diversity and EEO/MEO leaders (n = 10).

As in the last chapter, we note where groups differed significantly using a probability value of 0.05 on Fisher's exact test. For our non-DoD sample, significant differences were found between corporate interviewees and not-for-profit interviewees on business expertise; leadership skills; and EEO/MEO, AA, and diversity knowledge and skills. For the DoD sample, senior-level leaders differed from diversity and EEO/MEO leaders on analytical ability and skills. We discuss these differences in the respective sections below.

In the sections below, we describe each of the KSAO categories in more detail and cite percentages for subcategories within the categories in Table 3.1. We provide the subcategory percentages for the non-DoD sample in Table B.32 in Appendix B. As we stated in the last chapter, we do not provide a table with subcategory percentages for the small DoD sample because of the potential for identification by inference.

Interpersonal Skills

Regardless of interview sample, interviewees mentioned interpersonal skills the most often in their discussions of KSAOs for diversity leaders. Indeed, research has found that interpersonal skills are important for leaders in general (e.g., Avolio et al., 2003; Zaccaro, Kemp, and Bader, 2004).

Among interpersonal skills, *communication skills* came up the most often in our discussions. Seventy-two percent of non-DoD participants[2] and individuals from each DoD component mentioned communication skills. As one non-DoD interviewee stated, "Communication is the number one competency of any leader." Communication skills involve active listening, oral communication, written communication, assertive communication,[3] and nonverbal communication (Klein, 2009). These communication skills are necessary for many of the responsibilities of a diversity leader, particularly those involving stakeholder engagement. For example, several interviewees explained how excellent communication skills are essential for communicating the mission to stakeholders. As one DoD interviewee explained: "They [diversity leaders] need to communicate powerfully to articulate why diversity is a mission imperative." Diversity leaders also need to effectively articulate in writing and speech the organization's D&I vision, strategy, and initiatives. As a DoD interviewee noted: "He or she must be a great communicator, able to articulate what diversity is, and able to lead an organization in one direction." As a final example, diversity leaders need to communicate effectively to advise senior leaders and, as one DoD interviewee put it, "be able to write policy."

As noted by 49 percent of non-DoD participations, diversity leaders also need *influence and persuasion skills*. As with communication, leaders in general need these skills (Avolio et al., 2003). For diversity leaders, such skills involve persuading others to buy into diversity goals

---

[2] A higher percentage of corporate interviewees (96 percent) than not-for-profit interviewees (90 percent) cited interpersonal skills. However, this difference is not significant based on Fisher's exact test.

[3] Assertive communication is the "ability and willingness to state one's opinions, concerns, and desires in a manner that is direct and to the point without being offensive, demeaning, or hostile" (cited by Klein, 2009, p. 23).

and efforts. One DoD interviewee describes how diversity leaders have to "sell" D&I:

> You have to be [a] salesperson because you're constantly selling either to an audience that may feel they already know what you're talking about or that completely disagree with an idea you're going to share. You have to be able to understand the individual's or group's position and be able to sell them on the business case for diversity. In many cases, the un-selling of what people believe D&I is is harder than finding champions for it.

Diversity leaders not only need skills to lead others (e.g., influence and persuasion) but also need to be able to work well with others—to have good *collaboration and teamwork skills.* Indeed, 45 percent of non-DoD interviewees and 11 of the 16 DoD interviewees (69 percent) provided examples of KSAOs in this category, which they often referred to as general "people skills." Diversity leaders need to bring people together, facilitate groups, and collaborate to achieve their goals. These collaborative skills are important because many diversity leaders do not own the business units in the organization and have small staffs. They need to work well with other organizational leaders to implement D&I efforts. To be successful at collaboration and teamwork, diversity leaders need relationship-building skills. Just as with communication skills, relationship-building skills reflect several interrelated skills. Specifically, relationship-building skills require cooperation and coordination, intercultural sensitivity, service orientation (i.e., "customer service"), empathy,[4] self-presentation, social influence, and conflict resolution and negotiation (Klein, 2009). Our interviewees spoke to all of these skills in some fashion.

---

[4] We include empathy in our section on personality and attitudes. In the context of relationship-building skills, empathy is less about personality but more about "emotional intelligence," which is conceptualized as an ability. Specifically, emotional intelligence refers to the ability to perceive and process one's own and others' emotions to guide one's thinking and behavior appropriately (Mayer, Salovey, and Caruso, 2008). Emotional intelligence has been found to predict leadership outcomes above and beyond what is predicted by personality and general cognitive ability measures (see, for example, Rosete, 2007).

More than half of DoD interviewees and 28 percent of non-DoD interviewees also described the need for diversity leaders to be effective at *intercultural interactions*, which requires "sensitivity to others' ideas" and the "ability to appreciate individual differences among people and act appropriately based on that understanding and appreciation" (Klein, 2009, p. 25). Interviewees noted that skill at interacting with people from different cultures is especially important for implementing organizational change initiatives, which can affect the organization's cultural groups differently. Additionally, diversity leaders should be open-minded and interested in learning about other cultures to promote an inclusive environment. One DoD respondent discussed why this is important, stating:

> How do you build an environment where everyone can come in and serve and respect and care for each other? If the diversity management leader isn't inclusive, curious about understanding people, then that person [leader] shouldn't be there.

Our non-DoD interviewees (28 percent) also noted that diversity leaders need *political savvy*. Political savvy refers to skill at identifying and engaging key players in the organization to achieve "win-win" situations. For example, senior diversity leaders need political savvy to identify allies. As this non-DoD interviewee states:

> You need to figure out what leader will work with and support you. If you don't do this, what happens once the CEO changes? If he or she is the only one who is committed to diversity, when that CEO steps down, you're in trouble.

Although research suggests that conflict resolution and negotiation (or "conflict management") is a relationship-building skill, a relatively small portion of our interviewees and job postings identified conflict management as a skill. We speculate that many people—including our interviewees and the organizations posting jobs for diversity leaders—think of "conflict management" as part of broader competencies involving communication and relationship-building skills. Indeed, we did not find any "conflict management" competencies in the six diversity leadership competency models we reviewed. Instead, conflict management skill is described as part of such competencies as "communication" and "political savvy."

The job postings we examined tended to underscore the value of interpersonal skills. Analysis of the job posting results revealed that interpersonal skills and experience top the list of important KSAOs.

Business Expertise

Business expertise is the one KSAO category that received more attention from non-DoD diversity leaders than from the DoD diversity leaders we interviewed. We hypothesize that the reason for this difference is that a majority of the non-DoD diversity leaders come from the corporate world, which requires *intraorganizational expertise*—or a knowledge of the core business—to engage with internal stakeholders and link diversity efforts to the company's branding strategy, as this corporate leader describes:

> I think one of the first and most important competencies is the ability to learn and understand the business. It's important you understand not only the product that you're delivering but the political and social forces as well. To really be credible, you have to be able to talk about diversity in the context of that business or organization.

This is not to say that knowledge of the core business is not important for DoD diversity leaders, just that it may not be as critical as it is in the private sector. Indeed, all of the corporate leaders we interviewed identified the need to have business expertise, compared with only 67 percent of the not-for-profit (i.e., government and higher education) leaders we interviewed.

Another area of business expertise mentioned by 40 percent of non-DoD diversity leaders is *HR knowledge and experience*. Many senior diversity leaders said that having some background in HR—recruiting, development, talent management—is helpful but not required. That is, many interviewees felt that senior diversity leaders need not come from HR backgrounds to be successful. In fact, many interviewees (especially from the corporate sector) stated that coming from an "operational" background (i.e., from a core business function) may be even more important. As one corporate senior diversity leader puts it:

> [I] don't think you have to be an HR professional, but certainly knowledge of HR laws and ethics, compliance, know a little bit of a lot of things—I could be called upon by any leader in any areas to discuss diversity.

Leadership Skills

Leadership skills are critical to diversity leaders' jobs. At one level are *strategic leadership skills,* which were mentioned by 50 percent of DoD interviewees and 55 percent of non-DoD interviewees. The first part of strategic leadership is thinking strategically—being "visionary" and "innovative and creative." The second part is strategic planning—creating and implementing a vision and developing strategic plans and initiatives. As one non-DoD interviewee describes it, strategic planning requires knowing "how to move things above the line and below the line," where "above [the line] is your strategy, below [the line] is the people that are the most important in moving things."

According to some interviewees, strategic leadership is one category that is particularly important for diversity leaders but less so for EEO (and MEO) leaders. As discussed previously, diversity leaders are less involved with legal and compliance issues and more concerned with diversity vision and strategy, and therefore they need strategic leadership skills and experience. As one DoD interviewee described:

> So again I think you have to be somebody who can think strategically, because you have to be able to envision the end state. So thinking strategic to me is being able to have a vision, being able to have the communication skills to successfully espouse a vision.

In addition to strategic leadership skills, *general leadership skills* were also noted by 31 percent of DoD interviewees and 36 percent of non-DoD interviewees as necessary to succeed as a diversity leader. These skills include the ability to guide and motivate staff and to delegate responsibility. As one non-DoD interviewee noted, the general leadership skills are "typical skill sets" for leaders.

Even less commonly mentioned than general leadership skills are *organizational change management skills* (38 percent of DoD interviewees, 21 percent of non-DoD interviewees), although such skills are found in all of the competency models we reviewed. This area includes experience or skill at fostering, creating, or improving the organizational environment to make it more inclusive or innovative. The non-DoD diversity leaders we interviewed may have included change management skills as part of their discussion of strategic leadership skills. One non-DoD diversity leader's comments are illustrative: "[A diversity leader needs to] understand strategic planning and change management, not just what you'll read but how change process evolves over time through political dynamics." For DoD, change management is about the ability to adapt to achieve the mission. For example, one DoD interviewee described this as the ability to "adapt to manage change quickly—includes people, teams, culture, and challenges that may come about."

Interestingly, a higher percentage of not-for-profit interviewees from our non-DoD sample (90 percent) cited leadership skills than did for-profit (corporate) interviewees (65 percent). General leadership skills, in particular, received more mention by not-for-profit diversity leaders (52 percent) than corporate diversity leaders (23 percent). Although the result was not statistically significant, a higher percentage of not-for-profit diversity leaders (50 percent) than corporate diversity leaders (28 percent) mentioned general management responsibilities. This difference may partly explain why more not-for-profit interviewees than corporate interviewees cited general leadership skills.

With respect to leadership skills overall, the job postings we reviewed make more mention of general leadership and project management skills than do the interviews, which tended to focus more on strategic leadership skills. As noted in our discussion of comparisons between job postings and interview responses for roles and responsibilities, the job postings included some non-senior diversity positions that may require more project management. Our interviewees, by contrast, are mainly executive-level leaders who delegate project management to staff. This difference in leadership level may also explain why the job postings listed more organizational skills than the interviewees did; running the day-to-day operations of diversity programs requires attention to detail and other organizational skills. For non-DoD diversity leaders, the greater emphasis for personality requirements is on having the drive and will to lead change, since senior diversity leaders operate at a strategic level in the organization.

EEO/MEO, AA, and Diversity Knowledge and Skills

Interviewees from both DoD and non-DoD groups agreed that diversity leaders should have knowledge of *compliance and legislation*. This knowledge includes EEO (and/or MEO), civil rights, and AA legislation and policies. Among DoD interviewees, 63 percent—representing four of the five DoD components in the study—identified EEO/MEO knowledge as important for diversity leaders. However, DoD interviewees distinguished between the level of EEO/MEO knowledge needed by diversity leaders and EEO/MEO leaders. Specifically, EEO and MEO leadership positions require detailed knowledge of legal and compliance issues. Diversity leaders do not need as much detailed knowledge but must be able to craft a strategic diversity vision for the office. For many diversity leaders, their responsibilities do not include overseeing regulatory compliance.

Among non-DoD interviewees, a third (66 percent) of diversity leaders stated that knowledge of or skill in handling EEO, AA, and diversity concepts and issues is important for their line of work. For some diversity leaders, EEO knowledge and skill are important because they also have responsibilities for EEO compliance. Because more diversity leaders in not-for-profit organizations (48 percent) have responsibility for EEO and diversity than do non-DoD diversity leaders from the corporate world (23 percent), more not-for-profit leaders (86 percent) than corporate leaders (50 percent) described compliance and legislation expertise as important.

In addition to EEO (and MEO) knowledge, diversity leaders need knowledge about their primary subject matter—diversity and inclusion. About a third of DoD interviewees and 28 percent of non-DoD interviewees stated that a "deep" *knowledge of D&I concepts and issues* is important. One DoD interviewee described this type of knowledge as follows:

> Understanding of diversity in and of itself—certainly means race, gender, and ethnicity; understanding those dynamics and how to apply to work, leadership etc.; also understanding other types of diversity—language and culture, total force similarities between [a component] and civilians, and active duty. Since a lot falls under policy, you need to have familiarity with those systems and how changes in those systems might affect diversity; also, in an operational sense and how it affects operations.

A larger percentage of job postings (92 percent) specified EEO, AA, and diversity knowledge and skill than we found in our interviews (66 percent of non-DoD interviewees, 81 percent of DoD interviewees). The large difference between the percentage for job postings and the percentage for non-DoD interviews may stem from industry differences—specifically that the majority of job postings are from higher education, whereas the majority of our non-DoD interview sample is from private corporations. Higher-education institutions may have more legal restrictions in hiring and other employment actions (especially if those institutions receive government funding) and fewer resources to have separate EEO and diversity leadership roles. In contrast, the corporate world has more legal employment flexibility than higher-education and government institutions and more resources to create separate EO leadership and diversity leadership positions. These organizational differences may explain why the job postings include more mention of EEO, AA, and diversity knowledge and skill.

Personality and Attitude

Although very few of our DoD interviewees mentioned personality attributes or attitudes as important, 64 percent of the non-DoD diversity leaders described one or more personality characteristics as important to their jobs. Of the personality characteristics listed, being *driven or motivated* to persist was the most common across both samples (25 percent of DoD interviewees, 38 percent of non-DoD interviewees). Interviewees explained that they have to persuade others to take up D&I efforts—to buy in. In the process, many interviewees noted that they face pushback so they have to be motivated to push past setbacks. More than one non-DoD interviewee described having the courage to speak up:

> [A diversity leader needs to have the] ability to influence, and then managerial courage. By that I mean taking a stance, speaking up and speaking out, teaching others how to speak up and speak out. Don't be afraid to speak what the metrics are indicating. Be comfortable being the nudger, or bringing up topics that make people uncomfortable.

> You have to have courage. I say courage—know when to say "no," say "yes," and know when to speak up. If you are afraid to speak up, you'll miss ideas that come up. My job [is] to let them [leaders] know up front what the big picture looks like, to give them initiatives. My job is to tell the truth of the story from the numbers, complaints, any reports.

Other personality characteristics mentioned by our non-DoD interviewees include *adaptability* (17 percent), *empathy* (15 percent), *being detail oriented* (15 percent), and *integrity* (11 percent).

In addition to personality characteristics, several of our non-DoD interviewees (32 percent) argued that being *committed or passionate about diversity* helps senior diversity leaders perform well. This commitment can come from a moral place, as one non-DoD interviewee noted:

> [O]ne of the big pieces of being able to do this work effectively is to have the passion and commitment, and most people in this role have this towards the moral imperative of this type of work.

Although not listed as a primary competency in the majority of models we reviewed, commitment to diversity is listed in one model for diversity executives (Dexter, 2010, p. 5). It is described as follows:

> Certainly, the CDO should be committed to diversity both as a value in its own right and as an engine of better business perfor-

mance. That commitment includes maintaining expertise in the full spectrum of diversity, from cross-cultural sensitivity to the ability to define what constitutes an inclusive workforce, to the ability to make diversity a concrete reality in the business.

Perhaps because commitment to diversity can be viewed as a means to an end (i.e., in order to drive change), it does not get its own competency. However, we find it important to mention because this commitment may be more difficult to develop in a senior-level leader and may require explicit consideration when selecting people for senior diversity leadership positions.

Analytical Abilities and Skills

Analytical abilities and skills were a less frequent area of KSAOs identified across both of our interview samples (38 percent of DoD interviewees, 36 percent of non-DoD interviewees). This KSAO category relates to *abilities and skills involving analysis, research, and interpreting data or information.* Although this category was mentioned less frequently overall, six out of the ten DoD diversity and EEO/MEO directors we interviewed noted its value for diversity leaders. For example, one DoD diversity and EEO/MEO director emphasized the importance of experience with analytics:

> Without that understanding of analytics, [it's] more of a challenge to articulate where you're going.

Similarly, another DoD diversity and EEO/MEO director stated that a background in analytics aids a diversity leader in communicating with stakeholders:

> You have to be an example of what it is you're preaching, be able and credible enough to be able to discuss the statistic piece of it, the demographic piece of it, the evening news piece of it.

Interestingly, none of the senior DoD leaders we interviewed identified analytic abilities and skills when asked about desired KSAOs for diversity leaders. This was the only category of KSAOs in which a clear difference emerged between the responses of senior DoD leaders and DoD diversity and EEO/MEO directors. It is possible that the diversity and EEO/MEO directors have had more experience with analytical tasks and, therefore, see the value in analytical skills for diversity leaders. However, we did not ask interviewees about their own related skills and experience.

For non-DoD diversity leaders, analytical ability and skills were described in terms of understanding and applying diversity metrics to address diversity issues in the organization and move D&I efforts forward. The senior diversity leader may have a staff member who runs analyses, but, as one non-DoD respondent noted, "the leader needs to know where is the organization and what metrics are meaningful for showing evidence or lack of progress."

Consistent with the importance of analytical ability and skills, all but one of the competency models we reviewed includes a "results orientation" competency that involves the ability to ensure that D&I efforts contribute to organizational goals. To demonstrate the results from D&I efforts, the diversity leader must be able to design and develop appropriate metrics and convey results from metrics (which requires an understanding of how they work).[5]

KSAOs with Limited or No Mention in Interviews but Relevant to Diversity Leaders

Despite overlap in KSAOs identified by interviewees and those found in diversity leadership competency models, some KSAOs that the literature suggests are relevant to diversity leadership effectiveness received little or no mention by our interviewees. Of particular note, only a few interviewees explicitly referenced critical thinking and problem-solving skills, which appear across several competency models for diversity leaders. Similarly, all of the diversity leader competency models stress the diversity leader's role as a change agent. However, only 38 percent of our DoD interviewees and 21 percent of non-DoD interviewees

---

[5]   Hays-Thomas and Bendick (2013, p. 201) argue that many D&I practitioners have skill gaps in the area of analysis and evaluation. They recommend voluntary standards for D&I professionals, including standards for analytical skills.

discussed change management skills. Moreover, multicultural competence was not explicitly mentioned. However, interviewees' discussions of commitment to diversity, knowledge of D&I, intercultural interaction skills, and change management skills allude to the three main aspects of multicultural competence. These three main aspects are (1) awareness of one's biases, values, and assumptions; (2) understanding of other cultures and perspectives of those in those cultures; and (3) ability to respond appropriately to opportunities and challenges of diversity in the workplace (Cox and Beale, 1997; Chrobot-Mason, 2003).

We cannot know for sure why our interviewees made little or no mention of certain KSAOs that receive more prominence in the literature. The open-ended question format does not allow such an analysis. For example, if we had prompted them about problem-solving skills, we suspect many would have said that they were important for diversity leaders. Other research methods could be used in the future to address this limitation. For example, Hays-Thomas, Bowen, and Boudreaux (2012) demonstrated how a critical incident technique could be used to identify a preliminary set of skills related to diversity effectiveness in organizations. This technique involves asking individuals to describe work situations (i.e., "critical incidents") that demonstrate effective performance or ineffective performance. Trained researchers rationally sort the incidents to identify themes, in this case, of diversity skills. Although it has its own limitations, critical incidents can offer richer depictions of the work environment and allow for identification of KSAOs related to both effective and ineffective performance.

Summary

To execute their primary roles and responsibilities, diversity leaders require a host of KSAOs. Foremost are interpersonal skills, particularly those involving communication. Senior diversity leaders need to communicate effectively with organizational members at multiple levels and with external stakeholders, such as customers and suppliers. Knowledge of EO (and MEO) and diversity theory and practice is also desirable and, in some cases, required. To have the credibility within the organization and knowledge of how to effect change, diversity leaders also require business expertise and leadership skills. Diversity leaders also describe the need for critical thinking and problem-solving skills to develop and implement diversity metrics that will help demonstrate the return on investment of D&I efforts. Finally, personality and attitude toward diversity are key ingredients for effective diversity leadership. To sell organizational leaders and the workforce on their D&I visions, strategies, and efforts, diversity leaders need a "thick skin" and the ability to persist past setbacks in their plans.

CHAPTER FOUR

Selection and Development of KSAOs for Diversity Leaders

In the last chapter, we presented findings on the KSAOs needed by diversity leaders to be successful in their jobs. Because these diversity leadership positions exist at a senior level in DoD (GS-15 or O-6 equivalent), most of the KSAOs are needed by diversity leaders on day 1 of the job. This means that DoD would need to select individuals with higher levels of the KSAOs for diversity leader positions. However, DoD generally develops its own leaders, particularly in its military workforce. If DoD plans to grow its own diversity leaders, the malleability of diversity leader KSAOs is an important factor to consider because KSAO malleability directly affects whether a KSAO can be developed through training or experience.

This chapter begins with a brief discussion of KSAOs needed by different levels of leadership. We follow with a discussion on the malleability of managerial and leadership KSAOs, which provides context for which KSAOs are amenable to training and education interventions (i.e., professional development). We then move to a discussion of the types of professional development experiences that might contribute to successful diversity leadership. For this discussion, we rely primarily on results from our interviews with DoD and non-DoD diversity leaders. Finally, we briefly describe the educational content offered in nine diversity education programs at six higher-education institutions. This discussion is intended to assist DoD if it were to provide formal D&I education to its (future) diversity leaders.

Leadership KSAOs by Organizational Level

If DoD is to grow its own diversity leaders, DoD will need to know what KSAOs are required by leaders at different organizational levels. To address the limited research on leadership KSAO requirements at different organizational levels, Mumford, Campion, and Morgeson (2007) proposed and tested a model of leadership skills based on a *strataplex*, where *strata* refers to layers and *plex* refers to segmentation (categories). Specifically, Mumford, Campion, and Morgeson proposed that four ordered categories of leadership skills requirements— cognitive, interpersonal, business, and strategic—are layered such that higher-order skills, like strategic skills, are needed relatively more by senior leaders than by mid-level and junior leaders. The authors tested their model through a survey of junior, mid-level, and senior managers in a U.S. federal government agency. The model was mostly supported, although there were no statistically significant differences between strategic and business skill requirements.

Hays-Thomas et al. (2012) also proposed a preliminary model of skills for employees at different organizational levels, with a focus on skills for diversity effectiveness. Through a critical incident technique, they identified a set of values, knowledge, and skills for line staff, middle managers, and executives. Although there is overlap in content across the three organizational levels (e.g., all three levels require self-awareness), some content is unique to each organizational level or only covers two adjacent organizational levels (e.g., both middle managers and executives need knowledge of organizational structure, but line staff do not). Middle managers need several skills that would fall under the interpersonal skills KSAO category: active listening, ability to relate, persuasion, and conflict resolution. Executives have fewer specific skill areas but are expected to model diversity behaviors, have tact, and anticipate problems. They also need to develop diversity plans, which falls under strategic leadership. Although this study does not offer a complete model of diversity skills by organizational level, it provides insights into the differences in position requirements.

The main implication of these studies is that leadership KSAO requirements vary by organizational level, with senior leaders (e.g., executives) needing more strategic and business skills than do more junior personnel. However, some skills are foundational, meaning that everyone needs them. The importance of this type of work is that it suggests that development interventions should be timed with appropriate points in an individual's career trajectory.

Malleability of Leadership KSAOs

One of the questions we sought to address with this study is what KSAOs are amenable to training or education—that is, which KSAOs are malleable in adults versus those KSAOs that are more difficult to gain and thus will need to be focused upon during selection. To answer this question, we reviewed scientific literature on KSAO malleability, with a focus on KSAOs tied to management and leadership. We use the management and leadership KSAO literature because little research has focused on the developability of KSAOs in the D&I leadership context. We follow with discussions of the malleability of KSAO example categories: interpersonal skills, critical thinking and problem-solving skills, and multicultural competence. We use these KSAO categories as examples of complex skill sets that have been shown to be amenable to some change in adults but would take significant time and resources to modify significantly. We complete this section with our conclusions about the development potential of each KSAO category.

Domain Model of Managerial Competencies

Theories about KSAO malleability ultimately tie to theories of learning, motivation, and human development (Hogan and Warrenfeltz, 2003). Learning can be defined in two basic ways: (1) building new or more elaborate mental models (cognitive change) and (2) changing behavior after experience (skill development). Both learning definitions are relevant to leadership in that leaders hold mental models for their own and others' expectations for performance, and these mental models affect their behavior (Hogan and Warrenfeltz, 2003).

Hogan and colleagues (Hogan and Warrenfeltz, 2003; Hogan and Kaiser, 2005) proposed a "domain model of competencies" for effective leaders. They argue that all leadership competencies fall into four domains that represent a "hierarchy of increasing trainability" (Hogan and Kaiser, 2005, p. 172). Table 4.1 provides a short description of the domains and examples of competencies that fall within the domains.

Two features of the domain model are worth noting. First, the malleability of the competencies (or KSAOs) in the domains is ordered from hardest to train (intrapersonal) to easiest to train (business). Intrapersonal "skills" largely reflect dispositional characteristics that begin to develop in humans at an early age. These intrapersonal skills involve one's core self-esteem, self-control, and attitudes toward authority. In contrast, business skills are largely technical in nature. Learning how to develop and manage a budget, for example, is largely a cognitive task that can be taught in formal and informal settings, such as management courses. Second, leadership skills build upon intrapersonal and interpersonal skills. Therefore, although leadership skills are more malleable than intrapersonal and interpersonal skills, individuals without foundational intrapersonal and interpersonal skills will struggle more at learning how to lead than individuals with those skills.

Table 4.1
Overview of Domain Model of (Managerial) Competencies

Domain	Description	Competency Examples
Intrapersonal	Internalized performance standards; can control emotions and behaviors	Courage, integrity, core self-esteem, perseverance, patience
Interpersonal	Social skills; ability to build and maintain relationships with others	Political savvy, negotiation, oral and written communication, customer focus
Leadership	Ability to influence and build teams	Communicating a vision, strategic talent management, motivating others, managing diversity
Business	Technical ability and knowledge to "plan, budget, coordinate, and monitor organizational activity" (Hogan and Kaiser, 2005, p. 173)	Business acumen, developing business strategy, quality decisionmaking, functional business skills

SOURCES: Adapted from Hogan and Warrenfeltz (2003) and Hogan and Kaiser (2005).

In general, the KSAO categories that our interviewees identified can fall into these four domains. Some of the KSAO categories are obvious: leadership skills from our interviews falls into the leadership domain. Slightly less obvious is where to place the KSAO category of EEO, AA, and diversity knowledge and expertise. Since most of this KSAO category refers to knowledge and expertise on compliance and legislation (technical skill), we argue that the category should be placed within the business domain. The personality and attitudes KSAO category mostly falls within the intrapersonal domain, as personality characteristics are largely dispositional attributes.[1] The analytical ability and skills KSAO category does not fall neatly into one of the four domains. Critical thinking and problem-solving skills should play a role in quality decisionmaking, which Hogan and Warrenfeltz (2003) put under the business domain. However, critical thinking and problem-solving skills should also help leaders address interpersonal challenges (interpersonal domain) and manage diversity (leadership domain).

Managerial Dimensions in Developmental Assessment Centers

Another line of research on management and leader development focuses on a tool for professional development of employees, particularly managers: developmental assessment centers (DACs). Unlike traditional assessment centers, which focus on identifying employees for selection, often for promotion to management, DACs focus on professional development. DACs should therefore focus on behavioral dimensions[2] that can be improved. Rupp et al. (2006) describe the challenge of identifying dimensions for DACs because of limited research on the malleability of dimensions. However, Thornton and Rupp (2005, p. 244) offer a preliminary scaling of the "developability" of dimensions and associated development or training methods. The scale has

---

[1] Commitment to diversity, which we describe as more of an attitude, could be more amenable to development. Cox and Beale (1997) argue that diversity competence, which includes a commitment to diversity, is developable.

[2] Behavioral dimensions are groups of "behaviors that are specific, observable, and verifiable, and that can be reliably and logically classified together" (Thornton and Byham, 1982, p. 117). They are akin to competencies but are ones that meet the requirements noted in the definition (e.g., observable).

five levels, ranging from "nearly impossible to develop" to "somewhat easy to develop." The category of "nearly impossible to develop" is not associated with any training methods. The next two categories, "very difficult to develop" and "difficult to develop," are associated with long-term and extensive training and education, as well as counseling and mentoring. The two easiest-to-develop categories, "reasonable possibility to develop" and "somewhat easy to develop," are aligned with low-fidelity training methods, such as lectures and readings.

Similar to Hogan and colleagues (Hogan and Warrenfeltz, 2003; Hogan and Kaiser, 2005), Thornton and Rupp's (2005) scaling suggest that intrapersonal characteristics, like personality, are very difficult to develop. Specifically, Thornton and Rupp place conscientiousness, a personality characteristic, in a category of "very difficult to develop." Likewise, Thornton and Rupp put interpersonal skills and leadership skills in the next category of "difficult to develop"; this scaling of personality, followed by interpersonal and leadership skills, follows the order cited by Hogan and colleagues. Problem-solving techniques, planning and organizing techniques, and listening skills are in the second-easiest category of "reasonable possibility to develop," and non-verbal communication is given as an example of "somewhat easy to develop."[3]

Because of the limited research on developable dimensions for DACs, Gibbons et al. (2006) turn to the training and development literature to look for evidence of the developability of 16 common managerial dimensions. They group the 16 dimensions into four clusters: (1) problem solving (e.g., creativity), (2) approach to work (e.g., planning and organizing, adaptability), (3) communication (oral and written), and (4) relational (e.g., leadership, conflict management skills). Their summary of the literature is that it is "not entirely satisfactory as a basis for identifying dimensions suitable for DACs" (p. 109). However,

---

[3]   Hogan and colleagues place written communication in the interpersonal skills category (difficult to develop), whereas Thornton and Rupp put "nonverbal communication" in the easiest-to-develop category. This difference demonstrates the variety of communication skills and their differing degrees of complexity.

they note that the available evidence suggests that all dimensions can be developed "to some extent" (p. 109).

Rupp et al. (2006) and Gibbons et al. (2006) also discuss the importance of assessing how those being targeted for interventions like DACs think about the developability of dimensions or competencies. They cite evidence from training literature that if training participants do not believe something can be changed (i.e., it is fixed), they are less receptive to the training. Gibbons et al. surveyed 139 managers about the perceived importance and developability of the 16 traditional managerial competencies, as well as four nontraditional competencies that other literature suggests should be relevant for managers.[4] Overall, the managers considered all dimensions to be at least somewhat important for managers. These managers also thought that most dimensions were at least somewhat developable, with the exceptions being creativity and motivation.

Overall, literature on the developability or malleability of managerial competencies and KSAOs suggests that personality and motivation are very difficult to develop; interpersonal skills and leadership skills are difficult to develop; and skills related to problem-solving, communication, and technical skills (e.g., business procedures) are the easiest to develop.

Examples: Improving Interpersonal Skills, Critical Thinking and Problem-Solving Skills, and Multicultural Competence

In this section, we discuss improving interpersonal skills, critical thinking and problem-solving skills, and development of multicultural competence. These are complex KSAOs that take time to develop but are not as difficult to change as dispositional characteristics, such as personality traits. We chose to focus on improving interpersonal skills, critical thinking skills, and problem-solving skills because they are of keen interest to educators and employers and are critical to success in education, work, and life in general (see, for example, Abrami et al.,

---

[4]   The four nontraditional competencies—fairness, cultural adaptability, emotion management, and readiness to develop—are tied to the construct of multicultural competence, which we argue is important for diversity leaders.

2008). We selected multicultural competence as an example because of its centrality to the D&I domain; multicultural competence touches many KSAOs identified in our study, including intercultural interaction skills, change management, and commitment to diversity.

Interpersonal Skills

As previously discussed, interpersonal skills represent two main categories of skills: communication and relationship-building. According to Hogan and Warrenfeltz (2003), these skills build upon intrapersonal characteristics, notably personality characteristics. In a recent meta-analysis (a statistical summary of research findings across studies) Klein (2009) found that all "big five" personality factors—agreeableness, conscientiousness, emotional stability, extraversion, and openness to experience—are positively correlated with interpersonal skills. Extraversion (i.e., preferring social interactions, being "outgoing") had the strongest relationship with interpersonal skills. This result is not surprising, given that people who are extraverted seek social interactions and are motivated to have successful interpersonal interactions.

Although personality characteristics change over the life course (Roberts, Walton, and Viechtbauer, 2006), these changes are not so large and volatile as to suggest that a single low-impact event could significantly alter personality. To the extent that interpersonal skills are influenced by personality, a single training or education course is not likely to have large effects on interpersonal skills. However, factors other than personality likely influence the development of interpersonal skills, and there is some evidence that interpersonal skills can improve with instructional intervention. Specifically, behavioral modeling techniques—in which an instructor explains the interpersonal behaviors to learn, models the behaviors, and provides feedback to the learner on his or her performance of the behaviors—can improve interpersonal knowledge and skills (Klein, 2009). Therefore, interpersonal skills training could be included as part of the development of future diversity leaders.

Critical Thinking and Problem-Solving Skills

Although our interviewees did not explicitly reference critical thinking or problem-solving in their discussions of diversity leader KSAOs, research on leadership KSAOs highlights the importance of problem-solving and critical thinking for leadership effectiveness. For example, based on Mumford et al.'s (2000) model of leadership effectiveness, Connelly et al. (2000) showed that Army officers' leadership knowledge, complex problem-solving skills, and social judgment skills predicted the quality of their proposed solutions to complex leadership problems and their career achievement. Research suggests that problem-solving skills can be developed: In their review of the training and development literature, Gibbons et al. (2006) cite studies showing the effectiveness of different methods for developing aspects of problem-solving skills, such as divergent thinking.

In her review of cognitive development in adulthood, Halpern (2004) cites the importance of leaders' ability to engage in critical thinking, which Abrami et al. (2008, p. 1102) define as the "ability to engage in purposeful, self-regulatory judgment." Leaders need critical thinking skills to address the increasing complexity of their environments. Indeed, the Army has recognized a need for critical thinking among its officers since at least 2001; as a result, the Army Research Institute has conducted or funded efforts to develop critical thinking methods and tools for the Army (Leibrecht et al., 2009).

Although there is some debate in the literature on critical thinking as to whether critical thinking skills can be generalized across subject areas (e.g., from math to history), a recent meta-analysis (Abrami et al., 2008) suggests that instruction with critical thinking as a learning objective separate from the subject area content can improve critical thinking in students. Specifically, the meta-analysis shows that "mixed method" instructional designs, in which critical thinking is taught as a separate instructional block within a subject-based course (e.g., teaching formal logic skills as part of an algebra course), provide the highest average improvement in student critical thinking. Instruction that is designed to increase critical thinking absent of any subject matter immersion (i.e., a "general" method) and instruction that explicitly encourages critical thinking as part of subject-matter instruction (i.e., an "infusion" method) also increase critical thinking, but to a lesser extent than mixed methods. An "immersion" method, in which critical thinking is merely a "by-product of instruction," performs worse on average than the other instructional methods (Abrami et al., 2008, p. 1121). For developing future diversity leaders, the implication of this line of research is that critical thinking instruction can be taught within other courses, such as general leadership courses or those that teach specific business skills.

Multicultural Competence

Although not singled out as a main KSAO in our interviews, several interviewees mentioned topics related to multicultural competence. The research literature on multicultural, or diversity, competence describes it as a learning process or developmental process, beginning with awareness of oneself, moving to an understanding of the perspectives of other cultures and the barriers that they may face, and continuing to the development of strategies and techniques for handling diversity issues (Cox and Beale, 1997; Chrobot-Mason, 2003). The literature also cites the need for continual development of multicultural competence, involving competencies such as a willingness to learn continuously about one's cultural identity and seek experiences outside work to improve cultural understanding (Chrobot-Mason, 2003, p. 9). Because multicultural competence involves a development process, it cannot be developed in a single training event. Chrobot-Mason (2003, p. 12) explains:

> Although development of multicultural competencies may begin in management awareness training workshops, success ultimately depends on the manager's ability to assume personal responsibility for developing multicultural competence both inside and outside of the work context.

The implication for DoD is that formal training or education for multicultural competence is not sufficient. Indeed, available evidence on the effectiveness of diversity training suggests that diversity knowledge and attitudes can be improved but diversity-relevant skills and behaviors might not be improved (for reviews, see Curtis and Dreachslin, 2008, and Kulik and Roberson, 2008). DoD will need to foster an environment in which personnel are provided opportunities to develop and practice multicultural competence that include feedback to ensure that the lessons learned from opportunities are appropriate.[5]

Summary of Malleability of Diversity Leadership KSAOs

As described above, not all of the KSAOs for diversity leadership can be improved through training and education interventions. Those KSAOs that are intrapersonal (e.g., personality characteristics) should be the basis of selecting future leaders, whereas KSAOs from the business domain could be taught in management and leadership courses and therefore could be developed. Table 4.2 presents our conclusions about whether the KSAO categories for diversity leaders should be the focus of development for future diversity leaders, not current diversity leaders. Based on our review of job postings and our interviews, the expectation is that applicants for senior diversity positions should already have all of these KSAOs (i.e., KSAOs are the focus of selection, not development).

Professional Development for Diversity Leaders

DoD generally develops its own leaders, particularly on the officer side. OPM does not currently have a civilian job series that is specific to diversity professionals, but, based on a discussion with OPM, it may consider one in the future. If DoD were to develop a set of civilian positions to create a diversity professional track, it would be necessary for DoD to develop training requirements based on KSAOs that were amenable to training. Accordingly, we asked our non-DoD interviewees about their work experiences, including education and training, and asked our DoD interviewees what professional experiences they would recommend for diversity leaders in DoD. As noted earlier in the report, we chose a future-oriented approach for DoD interviewees because the focus of the DoD interviews was on defining the diversity

---

[5]   In her review of research on adult cognitive development, Halpern (2004) discusses how people tend to misjudge how well they understand complex subjects learned through unstructured experience. She recommends that on-the-job experiences be supplemented with instruction and "systematic informational feedback" to guide learners (p. 140).

Table 4.2
Conclusions About Development Potential of KSAOs for Future Diversity Leaders

KSAO Category	Development Potential
KSAOs from Interviews	
Interpersonal skills	Evidence suggests that these can be improved through interventions. However, individuals with poor interpersonal skills would likely not improve to the levels required for diversity leadership.
Business expertise	Technical aspects of business expertise, such as how to draft a policy document, can be trained. Business expertise based on deep knowledge of how the organization's core functions operate will likely require work experience to acquire.
Leadership skills	Technical aspects of leadership skills, such as identifying key organizational players to help promote diversity goals, can be developed over time through work experience. Leadership skills closely aligned with intrapersonal and interpersonal skills (e.g., knowing how to influence people) develop over time and may be less amenable to development.
EEO/MEO, AA, and diversity knowledge and skills	EEO/MEO, AA, and diversity topics can be learned through training, education, and on-the-job experience.
Personality and attitudes	Personality characteristics are among the most difficult KSAOs to modify. However, Cox and Beale (1997) suggest that diversity competence can be developed through learning processes.
Analytical abilities and skills	Analytical skills, such as data analysis, can be improved through training and education.
KSAOs Not Featured in Interviews	
Critical thinking and problem-solving	Critical thinking and problem-solving skills can be improved through training and education. However, these are complex skills that take time to develop. On-the-job experience with the types of problems faced in the area of D&I can be leveraged to assist future diversity leaders in enhancing their problem-solving skills.
Multicultural competence	Although training may increase awareness of diversity issues, developing multicultural competence is a learning process that takes time and requires some self-development.

leadership position as envisioned, which may differ from how it is currently defined.

Work Experience, Education, and Training

In our interviews with non-DoD diversity leaders, we first asked about their own experiences, education, and training to help identify whether certain backgrounds are associated with senior diversity leadership positions. Below, we list some key features of non-DoD interviewees' educational and job experience backgrounds:

- Most had college degrees (32 percent had a bachelor's degree, and 41 percent had a master's degree). Only 2 percent did not have college degrees.
- Subject areas for college degrees varied widely, with the most common subject areas being HR or organizational development (24 percent), business (18 percent), law (16 percent), and communications (16 percent).
- Sixty percent had held diversity positions in the past. Just over half (51 percent) had prior HR experience, and nearly half (49 percent) had experience in a business functional area (e.g., marketing). Only 27 percent had held EEO positions in the past.

Other than being college educated, these interviewees vary in their prior work and formal educational experiences. Although a majority of non-DoD interviewees (69 percent) had some type of diversity training or education experience, and 27 percent noted taking leadership courses, not all of that experience happens in a classroom. We also found a lot of variability in preferred or required educational and job experiences in the job postings. Although most of the positions required college degrees, the subject areas for those degrees ranged from business (30 percent) and HR (25 percent) all the way to physical sciences (2 percent). Similarly, preferred or required job experience varied, with the most common involving positions in diversity (55 percent), HR or organizational development (34 percent), higher education (32 percent), or leadership (30 percent).

Interestingly, a majority of non-DoD interviewees (67 percent) learned about diversity and leadership through interactions with peers and experts at conferences. Below, we list some of the more common courses and conferences mentioned, including the percentage of all non-DoD interviewees who mentioned each:

- the Conference Board (42 percent)
- Cornell University's diversity management program (22 percent)
- SHRM (18 percent)
- Diversity Best Practices (18 percent)
- Catalyst (16 percent)
- Defense Equal Opportunity Management Institute (DEOMI) courses (11 percent)
- Working Mother Media (11 percent)
- Linkage (9 percent)
- Multicultural Forum (7 percent)
- Georgetown University's diversity management program (4 percent).

Overall, both our DoD and non-DoD interviewees generally believed that successful diversity leaders come from a variety of educational and work backgrounds. However, many of the senior diversity leaders in the corporate world argued that prior experience in business operations gives them the credibility they need to effect change. This type of prior experience is also a common feature of the competency models we reviewed. In our interviews with DoD members, they also noted that regardless of specific content background, a diversity leader should be experienced enough to be taken seriously by other senior leaders.

Potential Training for DoD Diversity Leaders

As part of our interviews with DoD members, we asked them what education and training they would recommend for diversity leaders. Although there was no consensus on specific education or experience credentials, we identify some common themes from these interviews.

For example, interviewees identified several areas of knowledge and specific competencies desired in the discussions of KSAOs. They made similar recommendations for topics in which diversity leaders should receive education or training. Their suggestions for education and training topics include the following:

- EEO/MEO compliance and legislation
- unconscious bias
- management, leadership, and organizational culture
- human capital and personnel issues
- language and culture
- analytical tools and statistics.

Knowledge in these areas would benefit both diversity leaders and other diversity office staff. Given how many of our interviewees discussed EEO (and MEO) compliance and legislation in the context of KSAOs, it is not surprising that they also identified it as an important area for training. However, training for diversity leaders must go beyond the language of EEO. As one individual said:

> My biggest concern is the training and education piece. Right now, when we think of diversity as race, gender, and ethnicity, we don't think in terms of how we leverage those differences. Until you have training and are exposed to [different ways of thinking about diversity], you won't think about it.

Seven individuals discussed how diversity leaders should be aware of their own biases. This awareness was also described as part of the interpersonal skills that leaders need. One respondent commented that the topic of "unconscious bias," specifically, is important because:

> That's how your values are formed and how you bring that value formation into the workplace to make decisions. You have to be more consciously aware of what you're unconsciously assuming. It's okay to talk about race, ethnicity, gender. . . . That helps to stereotype-bust, and understanding your own stereotypes and how it impacts you as a leader.

Several interviewees identified courses in leadership as useful. One individual described his or her own experience with an effective leadership course:

> CDOs not only have to take risks and be unafraid of change, but from an educational perspective understand leadership principles. I've taken transformation and change leadership courses. I've learned about return on investment and diversity best practices.

Some interviewees specifically referred to aspects of leadership defined by OPM as essential for diversity leaders.

Several respondents thought it would be more valuable for diversity leaders to complete a comprehensive training program, perhaps with an associated credential or certification, rather than a selection of disparate courses. One interviewee who expressed this opinion noted:

> I don't think people should go out and take a variety of classes. Instead, DoD could create this itself at DEOMI and could say [that] if you got the job you need to complete this course in six months. Right now, there is no requirement for any training. They could build this in-house by defining the competencies needed for the positions and expectations. I would suggest they also have online courses and reoccurring classes, including webinars.

Consistency in training across leaders and other diversity staff emerged as a theme. Some interviewees suggested that training and education consistency could be achieved by developing a certification program. Specifically, many interviewees would like to see DoD develop its own diversity management training and, possibly, a certification process through DEOMI.

Interviewees mentioned a few exemplary courses in leadership and/or diversity management that would be beneficial for diversity leaders:

- Georgetown University's diversity management program
- Cornell University's diversity management program
- SHRM

- Reserve Component National Security Course (at Joint Senior Leadership War College)
- Joint Military Course (at National Defense University)
- DEOMI EO adviser core course
- Leadership Training Awareness Seminar (at DEOMI).

Many of these are consistent with some of the courses mentioned by our non-DoD diversity leaders. Regardless of whether a standard diversity certification is required of diversity leaders, DoD interviewees generally thought that continuing education, whether at external conferences or through in-house courses, was important.

Diversity Education Programs at Higher-Education Institutions

Because our interviews did not provide consensus on training and education content for diversity leaders, we reviewed publicly available information on a small sample (n = 9) of diversity programs[6] offered by six higher-education institutions. Below, the six institutions are listed in alphabetical order, along with their programs:

- Cleveland State University, College of Sciences and Health Professions
  - graduate certificate in diversity management/certification as a diversity professional
  - master's degree in diversity management/certification as a diversity professional
- Cornell University, School of Industrial and Labor Relations
  - diversity management certificate
  - Cornell Certified Diversity Professional/Advanced Practitioner (CCDP/AP) program
  - EEO professionals certificate

---

[6] One program is for EEO professionals. We include it to provide a fuller picture of the offerings at the institution (Cornell).

- Georgetown University, School of Continuing Studies
  - strategic D&I management certificate
- Mississippi State University, College of Arts and Sciences
  - diversity certificate
- Rutgers University, School of Management and Labor Relations
  - D&I in the workplace certificate
- University of Houston, Bauer College of Business
  - diversity management certificate program.

We provide more details about our selection of these programs (methodology) and the characteristics and content of the programs in Appendix C. Here, we provide a brief overview of themes for program characteristics and course content. The information on these programs is current as of fall 2013.

Program Characteristics

Most of the nine programs are certification programs designed for diversity professionals. Most of the programs have anywhere from four to nine courses, although Cleveland State University's master's degree program has 13 courses. Most of the programs last between 15 and 24 months, although the University of Houston program can be completed in as little as 4.5 days.

Most programs are only offered in residence. The two exceptions are Mississippi State's program (online only) and Rutgers' program (online or residence). Unlike venue, programs vary quite a bit in tuition costs. One-third of programs cost $5,000 or less, another third cost between $5,000 and $10,000, and the last third cost more than $10,000. Finally, programs differ in terms of admissions requirements, although five of the nine programs require at least a bachelor's degree. Two programs require a minimum number of years of experience in diversity roles: three years for Cornell's CCDP/AP and two years for the University of Houston's program.

Course Topics

We identified four course topic categories: (1) EO/AA, (2) diversity, (3) HR, and (4) skills and practical applications. Both EO/AA and diversity courses are the most common (eight out of nine programs for each). The most common type of EO/AA course covers legal compliance. Two less common types of EO/AA courses cover complaints/investigations and harassment/discrimination. Diversity courses are more varied, with the most common type of course covering theory and history, such as the history of the civil rights movement in the United States. Courses on change management/diversity initiatives and strategies are offered in over half of the programs. Less common diversity course topics include managing diversity (e.g., affinity) groups (44 percent), topics tied to specific groups (e.g., women; 33 percent), and supplier diversity (22 percent).

HR courses and courses designed to provide skills and practical applications are available in seven of nine programs. The most common HR courses cover recruiting and staffing for a diverse workforce and retention issues related to diversity. Less common are courses on training and professional development, including how to deliver training. Courses related to skills and practical applications vary but address any number of "soft" or "hard" skills that diversity practitioners need, such as skills related to communication, data analysis, group facilitation, budgeting, and leadership. These skill areas match many of the KSAOs identified by our interviewees as important for diversity leaders.

Summary

A major policy question regarding the key KSAOs identified for diversity leaders is whether they need to be selected or can be developed. That is, can DoD create diversity leaders, or does it need to select them? The answer is "both." Some KSAOs, such as personality characteristics (e.g., being "driven"), are difficult to modify through training and would need to be identified in potential leaders through a selection process. In contrast, technical knowledge and skill, such as learning EEO and diversity concepts, can be taught in courses or at conferences.

In general, the diversity leaders we interviewed did not have consistent backgrounds or educational experiences. Instead, there seemed to be agreement that diversity leaders could have varied experiences.

That being said, interviewees agreed that diversity leaders need certain formal work and education experiences, particularly as diversity leaders are developed within DoD. Further, the growing number of diversity education programs at higher-education institutions may alter which formal experiences future diversity leaders consider important. Based on our review of nine diversity education programs, diversity leaders of the future may have formal education in topics related to EEO/AA, diversity, HR, and various skills needed to practice diversity management. Courses may cover topics such as EEO/AA compliance; diversity theory and history; change management; recruiting, staffing, and retaining a diverse workforce; communication skills; data analysis; and leadership. These course topics are worth consideration if DoD were to require formal education and training experiences for diversity leaders.

CHAPTER FIVE

Conclusions and Recommendations

In 2012, DoD published its strategic D&I plan. DoD components established D&I plans, as well as leadership positions to implement their plans. To determine what it takes to be successful in these leadership roles, ODMEO asked RAND to identify the key attributes and experiences needed for these positions. We used a job analytic approach to identify job demands (roles and responsibilities) and the KSAOs and professional experiences that might be needed to meet those demands. Our analytic approach relied on four key sources of information: (1) interviews with DoD diversity leaders, (2) interviews with non-DoD diversity leaders, (3) online job postings for diversity leader positions, and (4) leadership literature, including competency models for diversity leadership. We also examined which KSAOs are amenable to training and education interventions and reviewed a sample of diversity programs in higher-education institutions.

Although we used multiple information sources to strengthen our conclusions and recommendations, we were not able to validate empirically the KSAOs identified through these sources. For example, we were not able to correlate measures of the KSAOs with measures of diversity leader performance. However, the challenge of validating diversity leader KSAOs is not limited to our study; it is a challenge that the D&I field still struggles to address as well. To the extent that diversity leadership KSAOs align with those needed by leaders in general, we rely on prior research demonstrating the empirical validity of leadership KSAOs.[1] Therefore, in this chapter, we offer conclusions about diversity leader KSAOs with the acknowledgment that they have not been empirically validated. We also outline a three-step recommendation to guide policy on developing diversity leaders in DoD, which calls for additional refinement of KSAO requirements before implementing training and education.

Several KSAOs Are Preferred or Required to Perform Diversity Leader Roles and Responsibilities

Our DoD diversity leader interviews, non-DoD diversity leader interviews, and the online postings for diversity leader positions outside DoD provide significant overlap in the primary roles and responsibilities for diversity leaders. The major categories include those listed below:

- strategic leadership (including leading diversity programs and initiatives)
- stakeholder engagement
- tracking diversity trends
- HR-related activities.

Strategic leadership and stakeholder engagement are considered by our interviewees to be the most important types of roles and responsibilities for diversity leaders. They include such activities as advising the organization's top leadership and educating the organization's workforce on diversity goals, plans, and initiatives; working with suppliers, local communities, and other external stakeholders to ensure that the organization's diversity message is promulgated; and developing and communicating a D&I vision. Although considered by interviewees as less critical to diversity leader positions, tracking diversity trends is a necessary means by which diversity leaders benchmark their diversity initiatives and demonstrate the return on investment of the initia-

---

[1]   For a brief discussion of literature on validated leader KSAOs, see Avolio et al. (2003).

tives. Tracking diversity trends also helps diversity leaders to forecast workforce changes that their organization needs to adapt to in order to attract and retain talent. Along those lines, diversity leaders work with or within HR departments to provide a "diversity lens" for recruiting, hiring, and development practices. Indeed, some diversity leaders have direct responsibility for HR and talent management units or programs.

To perform these roles and responsibilities, diversity leaders would ideally have KSAOs that fall into these categories:

- interpersonal skills
- EEO/MEO, AA, and diversity knowledge and skill
- leadership skills
- business expertise
- personality and attitudes
- critical thinking and problem-solving skills
- analytical abilities and skills
- multicultural competence.

Regardless of source, interpersonal skills were mentioned the most often. Many diversity leaders do not own any of the core or operational business units in their organizations. Diversity leaders therefore need interpersonal skills to communicate and build relationships with people across the organization to gain the "buy-in" needed to implement their D&I strategies. They also need these skills to project the image of the organization as one that values diversity; this strategic messaging can help attract diverse talent, suppliers, and customers.

Diversity leaders also need subject-matter expertise, mainly knowledge of EEO (and MEO), AA, and diversity concepts and issues. The level of expertise that diversity leaders need depends on whether they have EEO or HR responsibilities. If they are responsible for EEO compliance, they will need more EEO compliance expertise than a diversity leader without this responsibility. Because many diversity leaders have budgets and staff, they also need general leadership skills (e.g., the ability to influence and build teams) and business expertise (e.g., the ability to develop and execute business plans).

Diversity leaders also benefit from certain personality character-istics and attitudes. Among those most commonly mentioned in our interviews and job postings, being driven or persistent was considered important. Diversity leaders are often trying to effect organizational change, which can be met with resistance by some organizational members. They need to persist in changing the resistance, or at least moving past it, to effect change. Moreover, diversity leaders need criti-cal thinking and problem-solving skills to deal with the complexities of organizational change. They also need analytical skills to develop and understand diversity metrics to track diversity trends. Finally, diversity leaders need multicultural competence to understand how to relate to people with other worldviews and develop action plans for identifying opportunities and addressing challenges to D&I in the organization.

Some KSAOs Can Be Improved Through Training and Education

Not all of the KSAOs for diversity leadership can be improved through training and education interventions for potential diversity lead-ers. Scholars have proposed a domain model of managerial compe-tencies that can encapsulate all leadership KSAOs (see Hogan and Warrenfeltz, 2003). The model's four domains—intrapersonal, inter-personal, leadership, and business—represent a hierarchy of trainabil-ity, with intrapersonal KSAOs being the hardest to train, and business KSAOs being the easiest to train. The implication is that KSAOs that are intrapersonal should be the basis of selecting future leaders, whereas KSAOs from the business domain could be taught in management and leadership courses and therefore could be developed. Similar efforts to identify malleable or "developable" leadership KSAOs are described in the literature on DACs. Thornton and Rupp (2005), for example, rate the difficulty of developing a sample of leadership KSAOs to help prac-titioners identify the types of KSAOs to include in DACs. Like Hogan and Warrenfeltz, Thornton and Rupp consider personality character-istics to be "very difficult to develop" and consider interpersonal skills and leadership skills to be "difficult to develop." Overall, the literature on the developability or malleability of managerial competencies and KSAOs suggests that personality and motivation are very difficult to develop; interpersonal skills and leadership skills are difficult to develop; and skills related to problem-solving, communication, and technical skills (e.g., business procedures) are the easiest to develop. Based on these and other findings, we summarized the development potential of the KSAO categories in our study (see Table 4.2 in the previous chapter).

Because of the variations in responses from our DoD interviewees about the separation of EEO/MEO and diversity positions, we do not offer a recommendation as to whether DoD should create a diversity professional track that is separate from the EEO/MEO professional track. However, if DoD were to develop a diversity leadership professional track, DoD should develop training and education criteria focused on the more malleable KSAOs. These include business expertise (e.g., developing policy documents, conducting barrier analyses, DoD budgeting processes); leadership skills (e.g., identifying key DoD players in promoting diversity initiatives); and EEO/MEO, AA, and diversity knowledge and skills (e.g., knowledge of EO compliance law and policy). Interpersonal skills, critical thinking and problem-solving skills, and multicultural competence can also be developed but will take more time and resources to develop than technical or functional knowledge and skills.

DoD Should Determine Training and Education Requirements for Diversity Leader Positions

There Is No Consensus on Work, Training, and Education Experiences for Diversity Leaders, but Some Themes Emerge

Our interviews with DoD and non-DoD diversity leaders did not identify specific backgrounds and experiences that diversity leaders might need to be successful. In fact, many of the interviewees suggested that people from a variety of work backgrounds could be successful. That said, experience in HR, personnel management, and corporate experience were described as useful by the DoD interviewees. Prior work experiences by our non-DoD interviewees matched two of the three experience types mentioned by DoD interviewees: Over half of non-DoD interviewees had prior HR experience (51 percent), and about half had business functional experience (49 percent). Prior business experience helps diversity leaders gain business expertise and, depending on the nature of their prior HR experience, can help with acquisition of EEO/MEO, AA, and diversity knowledge and skills.

DoD interviewees described several education and training topics that diversity leaders would benefit from learning. Topics include EEO compliance and legislation; unconscious bias; management, leadership, and organizational culture; human capital and personnel issues; language and culture; and analytical tools and statistics. A majority of the non-DoD interviewees have taken diversity training or education courses, although many of the interviewees commented that they learned about diversity and leadership issues at conferences.

Both DoD and non-DoD interviewees identified several courses, programs, and conferences that they had attended, had sent staff to attend, or would recommend. Both sets of interviews included mention of Georgetown's and Cornell's diversity management programs, SHRM courses, and DEOMI courses. Some DoD interviewees also noted courses provided by military education institutions. Because several of the non-DoD interviewees come from the corporate world, several mentioned the Conference Board. The differences in industry and prior work experience likely contribute to the differences among our interviewees' recommendations for training and education of diversity leaders.

Because our interviews did not yield recommendations for specific training and education programs for diversity leaders, we also reviewed the content of nine diversity education programs offered by six civilian higher-education institutions. These programs offer courses in four topic areas: (1) EEO/AA, (2) diversity, (3) HR, and (4) skills and practical applications. At least half of the programs offer an EEO/AA legal course (Topic 1); diversity theory and history (Topic 2); change management and diversity initiatives (Topic 2); recruiting and staffing (Topic 3); and retention (Topic 3). These topic areas are consistent with some of the KSAO areas identified as part of this study. Appendix C provides a list of courses currently offered by these civilian universities.

We Recommend Three Steps for Determining How to Train and Educate Future DoD Diversity Leaders

Based on the study findings, instead of prescribing a single course of action, we have developed a three-step plan of action to assist DoD in deciding how to develop future diversity leaders with a focus on training and education.[2] Although conducting the analysis to inform the three steps is beyond the scope of the current study, we recommend these steps as a way forward for DoD's efforts to develop its future diversity leaders.

Step 1: Determine Whether There Should Be a Separate Professional Development Track for D&I Personnel. Prior to deciding the specific means by which future D&I leaders should be trained and educated, DoD will first need to decide whether to establish a distinct professional development track for civilian and military personnel with D&I responsibilities or to create a developmental pathway for a larger group of personnel who perform D&I, EEO/MEO, and perhaps other HR-related activities over the course of their careers. Not only is this step important in terms of instilling a sense of professional identity, but it also has practical implications when it comes to ascertaining the size of the cohort that will need to be trained and the types of training, education, and experiences that should be provided at different stages of a person's professional development.

Step 2: Determine Training and Education Requirements. Once the decisions about professional development track(s) have been made, DoD must develop relevant training and education requirements. As noted in the last chapter, certain KSAOs are more amenable to development (e.g., EEO/MEO knowledge) than others (e.g., personality characteristics). Of the KSAOs that are amenable to development,

---

[2] Professional development goes beyond formal training and education and can include such activities as mentoring, coaching, and on-the-job learning. However, we focus on formal training and education because of the potentially significant resources involved in offering training and education and the complexity of decisions for determining training and education requirements.

some are rather generic (e.g., interpersonal skills), and some are more specialized (e.g., EEO/MEO, AA, diversity knowledge and skills). This latter distinction can be important when selecting a training or education provider. On the one hand, in-house training and education, in which the customer has considerable control over instructional content, is normally more appropriate for the development of a highly specialized skill. On the other hand, external providers with a record of providing quality instruction are usually better at imparting knowledge and skills that are useful across a range of job categories (Galanaki, Bourantas, and Papalexandris, 2008).

Although this report has focused on identifying KSAOs for diversity leaders, training and education requirements should be established for more-junior personnel to ensure that those who rise to the top have acquired the skills and knowledge at the appropriate points in their careers. Beyond that, DoD must calculate how many personnel overall need to be trained and educated and what types of training and education experiences they need at each career stage. The final output of this step will be the number of personnel at different organizational levels who require generic and specialized training and education to prepare them for diversity leadership roles.

Step 3: Determine Means for Fulfilling Training and Education Requirements. To satisfy the education and training requirements resulting from the previous step, DoD will need to decide the means for providing training and education for future diversity leaders. A major decision for DoD is whether to insource or outsource the training and education. Insourcing would require DoD to provide instruction, whereas outsourcing would involve non-DoD (external) providers. External providers may come from non-DoD governmental organizations that offer D&I training and education or from nongovernmental sources (e.g., D&I experts from academia, for-profit training vendors). Although there are many purported costs and benefits associated with insourcing and outsourcing, little empirical evidence is available to point to which factors are useful in making decisions about whether to outsource training. An exception is a study by Galanaki, Bourantas, and Papalexandris (2008), in which 100 HR directors in Greece were surveyed about their companies' decisions to outsource.

Galanaki, Bourantas, and Papalexandris tested decision models involving factors that affect perceived benefits of outsourcing, which in turn predict the decision to outsource. Companies that have invested heavily in their in-house training capability, are larger in size, and see training as a source of competitive advantage are less likely to perceive the benefits of outsourcing training. However, the availability of training in the external market increases the perceived benefits of outsourcing training. The existence of training in the external market was weighted more heavily in decisions to outsource than most of the other factors, except training as a source of competitive advantage when the skills are job-specific or organization-specific.

Other factors that DoD will need to consider when deciding how to offer training and education for future diversity leaders include the following:

- **course development:** use of existing courses, modification of existing courses, or development of new courses
- **time** requirements for courses
- **quality of instruction** (ideally measured by independent SMEs, such as accreditation organizations)
- **venue:** online, face to face at non-DoD locations (e.g., a brick-and-mortar academic institution), and/or face to face at DoD locations (e.g., DoD training locations, DoD work sites)
- **flexibility** in course modification (this will likely be lower when outsourcing)
- **development of an in-house training capability** (e.g., developing a train-the-trainer model with outside experts training DoD instructors)
- **instilling new ideas** into the organization (perceived as more likely to come from outsourcing; Galanaki, Bourantas, and Papalexandris, 2008)
- **financial costs:** tuition and fees for outsourced training; travel, room and board for offsite locations; course development costs if new courses are developed; instructor costs for in-house training; etc.

Unfortunately, none of these factors can be fit into a predetermined formula; they must be weighed in accordance with priorities set by DoD decisionmakers. Moreover, uncertainty will be higher in decisions involving new courses or programs than for those involving the use of existing courses and programs. For example, the cost of an existing course can be established relatively easily, assuming that one knows the number of students and their availability, but the costs of a newly developed course would need to be estimated. Furthermore, DoD must infer the quality of potential courses, either by reviewing courses that are similar to the ones desired or by evaluating the administrative and instructional reputation of the institutions or vendors willing to develop the new courses.

Final Remarks

Although many organizations are creating senior diversity leadership positions, the individuals who occupy them come from diverse professional backgrounds. Nonetheless, diversity leader roles involve KSAOs aligned with successful leadership in general: interpersonal skills, business expertise, general leadership skills, drive, and critical thinking skills. In addition to general leadership KSAOs, diversity leaders need to know their trade—namely, diversity (and EEO) theory and practice. They also need HR-related skills to understand how their organizations can attract, select, develop, and retain a diverse workforce and promote an inclusive climate. A variety of professional work, training, and educational experiences may support development of some of these KSAOs. Our study did not identify specific training and education programs, but our analysis of the content of diversity education programs identified such topic areas as EEO/AA, diversity, and HR.

Because of the limited guidance from our interviews on training and education for future diversity leaders, we laid out a three-step plan for determining how to train and educate future diversity leaders in DoD. This plan calls for DoD to first decide whether to create a separate D&I professional development track or to combine D&I with EEO/MEO and/or HR personnel into an integrated job series.

The plan then calls for DoD to determine the nature of training and education requirements in qualitative and quantitative terms. Finally, the plan requires DoD to ascertain how to provide the training and education to future diversity leaders. Ultimately, our plan will help DoD move forward in deciding whether to promote a specific D&I professional track as a pathway to senior diversity leadership positions.

Methodology

In the study described in this report, we employed a variety of information collection and qualitative data analysis activities. This appendix provides details on these methodological activities. We do not follow chapter order in presenting the methodologies but instead cover methodological topics from least to most involved in terms of time and resources. Specifically, we cover methodological topics in the following order:

- literature review
- job posting search strategy
- interview protocols
- content analysis of job posting and interview material
- codebook used in content analysis.

Literature Review

Search Strategy

The literature review focused on scholarly and other documentation (e.g., trade publications) on diversity management. We were specifically interested in finding and reviewing information for the following three content areas: (1) roles and responsibilities of senior diversity leaders, such as CDOs, (2) KSAOs or competencies of senior diversity leaders and diversity professionals, and (3) training or other professional experiences and credentials acquired by senior diversity leaders or diversity professionals. For each area, we used a multistep search strategy. We started with academic databases (e.g., Academic Search Complete), followed by Google Scholar, and then Google. If the initial search results yielded over 500 hits, we sorted the results by relevance and then searched through the first few hundred until we achieved saturation. If we found relevant documents, we used a forward search (snowballing) to identify additional sources of information. We supplemented our database searches and snowballing method with searches of websites from a select number of diversity organizations (e.g., Diversity Inc.) recommended by diversity experts.

Our search of the academic databases initially produced anywhere from 75 results (for KSAOs/competencies) to over 6,300 results (for diversity training and education). However, the large number of results yielded few relevant (50 or less) articles, books, or other scholarly reports. Our Google Scholar and Google searches initially yielded at least 100,000 results for most searches. As with our search of academic databases, few of the results from any given search were relevant. We also found significant overlap between the academic databases and Google Scholar and Google in terms of what we found to be relevant. Overall, we found thousands of pieces of information on the topic of diversity—particularly diversity training in the workplace—but few were relevant to the work of senior diversity leaders and other high-level diversity professionals.

Diversity Leader Competency Models

Our literature search yielded six competency models[1] specific to diversity leadership roles. Two of the models are designed for specific types of organizational settings: higher education and academic medicine. Because the models vary in descriptiveness and breadth, we do not describe them in detail here but provide an overview in Table A.1. In the table, we include competency model titles, how the models were developed, and the model's competencies or competency categories.

---

[1]   One of the competency models was developed by an OPM-led workshop of D&I experts across several federal agencies. Because the report is not publicly available, we do not cite it in our report.

Table A.1
Competency Models for Diversity Leadership

Title	How Model Was Developed	Competencies/Categories
CDO Competencies in Academic Medicine[a]	Based on a daylong session (CDO Forum) with 16 experts and follow-up interviews with 10 more experts on CDO role in academic medicine	Seven competency categories: • strategic vision and executive acumen • change management expertise and will • political savvy • persuasive communicator and framer of information • ability to navigate the culture of academic medicine • innovator's DNA • cultural intelligence and technical mastery of D&I strategy
Essential Competencies for Chief Diversity Officers[b]	Based on an executive search firm (Heidrick & Struggles) analysis of the roles of diversity executives among 307 Fortune 500 companies (out of 490 companies analyzed)	Seven competencies: • business acumen • leadership • change management • results orientation • building and maintaining credibility • ability to influence • commitment to diversity
Global Diversity and Inclusion Competency Model[c]	Developed based on data from the Conference Board Council on Workforce Diversity (and associated councils). Data collected via surveys with members of U.S. councils ($n = 67$) and a two-day workshop with members. Members of non-U.S. councils provided feedback on model.	Seven competency categories (27 competencies total): • change management • diversity, inclusion, and global perspective • business acumen • strategic external relations • integrity • visionary and strategic leadership • HR disciplines
Interactive Emerging Leadership Competency Model[d]	Developed by academics based on their review of other academics' leadership competency models and diversity management competency models	Five competencies: • diversity management • personal management • leadership • interpersonal management • actional management

Table A.1—Continued

Title	How Model Was Developed	Competencies/Categories
Key Attributes of CDO Candidates[e]	Developed by academics based on interviews with over 70 senior diversity leaders in higher education. The model focuses on attributes of CDOs in higher-education institutions.	Seven competencies: • technical mastery of diversity issues • political savvy • ability to cultivate a common vision • in-depth perspective on organizational change • sophisticated relational abilities • understanding of the culture of higher education • results orientation

SOURCES: [a] American Hospital Association Institute for Diversity in Health Management and Association of American Medical Colleges (2012). [b] Dexter (2010). [c] Lahiri (2008). [d] Visagie et al. (2011). [e] Williams and Wade-Golden (2007).

We also reviewed some of the general leadership literature to identify overlap in general leadership KSAOs and the competencies in the competency models described in Table A.1. We did not use a systematic approach to identify the general leadership literature, as they were not the primary focus of our literature search. We instead relied on leadership literature reviews and snowballing techniques to identify relevant research on KSAOs needed by leaders.

Job Posting Search Strategy

We searched employment websites for diversity leadership position postings listed between mid-December 2012 and early January 2013. Specifically, we searched general employment websites (e.g., Monster.com), as well as employment websites for positions in higher education (e.g., Chronicle.com), human resource management (e.g., shrm.org), and federal government (e.g., GovernmentJobs.com). We started the search using general terms, such as "diversity," "equal opportunity," "inclusion," "minority," and "multicultural affairs." If needed, we narrowed our search with such terms as "chief diversity officer" and "diversity director." We sorted search results by relevance and scanned the position descriptions. If there were over 500 results, we scanned until there were no longer promising results. Over 97,000 results were returned via search engines, most of which were redundant. We scanned nearly 1,100 postings and determined that there were 73 that were unique. We removed 20 postings after determining that the positions were not applicable to our study (e.g., "diversity supply manager"), resulting in 53 positions to analyze.

Interview Protocols

DoD Diversity and EEO/MEO Leaders
Identifying Participants
From August through October of 2014, we conducted semi-structured interviews over the phone with 16 DoD leaders (six senior leaders and ten diversity and EEO/MEO directors). We identified most of the senior leaders from their membership on the Defense Diversity Working Group (DDWG), which is primarily responsible for decisions regarding implementation of DoD's strategic D&I plan. The DDWG is supported by diversity and EEO/MEO working groups comprised of mostly O-6- or GS-15-level leaders of diversity or EEO/MEO offices and programs. Most of the ten diversity and EEO/MEO directors were members of these working groups, which provide component-specific diversity and EEO/MEO information and resources, such as demographic trends data.

Interview Procedures
Out of the 20 individuals we contacted, 16 granted interviews, for a response rate of 80 percent. Each interview lasted about an hour and was led by one researcher, who was accompanied by a note-taker. Some interviews were conducted via telephone, and some were conducted in person. Each interviewee was asked a series of questions about his or her roles and responsibilities, the roles and responsibilities of diversity leaders in DoD, the KSAOs needed by those leaders, how best to structure diversity offices in his or her component, and the component's

D&I plan. Note that we used the term "diversity management leadership" in our interviews to avoid confusion with diversity competencies for all types of leaders.

We used our expertise in job analytic techniques to guide the initial protocol design, which we decided to keep in an open-answer format to allow individuals to provide enough detail about roles, responsibilities, KSAOs, and other topics of interest. We submitted our protocols to ODMEO to benefit from their expertise in military culture vis-à-vis D&I and to ensure that we asked questions that could achieve the study goals. The inputs from ODMEO (e.g., questions about structure of diversity offices in DoD) were included in our protocol design.

Non-DoD Diversity Leaders
Identifying Participants
Our primary analysis focused on findings from interviews with CDOs and other senior diversity leaders in the public and private sectors. To address role and responsibility differences across organizations, we sought to identify senior diversity leaders from different types of organizations. We focused on four types of organizations: private sector (for-profit and not-for-profit), higher education, federal government, and state or local government. Within those four categories, we aimed to sample organizations of various sizes (based on number of employees), industries, and geographic locations within the United States.

We conducted searches for companies with CDOs or senior diversity leaders using general search engines (e.g., Google) and websites for diversity or human resource professionals (e.g., shrm.org, diversityinc.org) and through consultation with our sponsor's office. We identified 97 potential interviewees. A majority were in private-sector organizations (74 percent), followed by federal government agencies (13 percent), higher-education institutions (7 percent), and state or local government (5 percent). (Percentages do not total 100 because of rounding.)

To scope our effort, we limited our initial contact list to 40 individuals. We undersampled private-sector organizations and oversampled organizations from the other three categories. Unfortunately, we later discovered that nine of the 40 individuals had missing or outdated contact information or were no longer with their organizations. In

February 2012, we sent emails to invite the remaining 32 senior diversity leaders to participate in the study. At the bottom of each email, we included a letter of support from our sponsor with the goal of increasing participation.

Because of an initially low response, we emailed the remaining 57 individuals on our initial contact list. Of those, six individuals had missing or incorrect contact information, thus reducing our overall original contact list to 82 individuals. For all 82 individuals, we sent up to two reminder emails to those who did not initially reply.

At the end of our interviews, we asked interviewees if they would recommend other senior diversity leaders for the study. This snowball method produced an additional 15 contacts, a few of whom could be described as senior EEO leaders. In total, we contacted 97 individuals to participate in the study (82 from the original list plus 15 from the snowball method).

Interview Procedures

Of the 97 leaders we contacted, 47 agreed to participate in the study, resulting in a response rate of 48 percent. Interviews lasted anywhere from 30 minutes to just over an hour. Given the geographic dispersion of senior diversity leaders we interviewed, all of the interviews were conducted by phone. During each interview, one team member asked questions, while another took notes. Interviews were semi-structured and followed a similar format as the one used for DoD interviews, with the exception that the non-DoD interview protocol did not include questions about diversity office structure and was focused on the interviewees' current positions, not future diversity leadership positions.

Content Analysis

In this section, we describe our content analysis methods for the job postings, DoD interviews, and non-DoD interviews. In Appendix B, we provide tables with descriptions of the codes in our codebook and additional results from job postings and non-DoD interviews. For simplicity, we refer to the codebook for non-DoD interviews as the "CDO codebook."

Job Postings

We coded job posting content into several categories using an iterative process. Two team members who were experts in job analytic methods open-coded the posting content to identify relevant themes. The themes formed the basis of codes, which were then grouped into seven categories to develop a coding scheme. The categories are as follows:

- industry
- job title
- organizational relationships
- job roles and responsibilities
- education and training background (includes preferred and required qualifications)
- work experience (includes preferred and required experience)
- KSAOs needed for the position.

A third team member with expertise in content coding methodology used the coding scheme to code the job postings (using QSR NVivo 9 software). The two job analytic methods experts then independently reviewed the results. When the two experts disagreed about coding results, they met with each other and the coder to reach an agreement on the coding. Although there were few cases of disagreement, some of the content in the postings was too vague and could not readily be classified into one of the predetermined codes; vague content was placed into miscellaneous codes. Also, not all job postings provided content relevant to a given category; we counted those postings toward a *not mentioned* code for each category. To identify the most common themes, we tabulated the number and percentage of job postings coded for each category. We then looked for differences across industries and regions.

Interviews

Although our project tasks place the DoD leader interviews (Task 1) before the non-DoD leader interviews (Task 2), the non-DoD interviews were conducted first because of delays in getting approval to conduct the DoD interviews. Therefore, the coding methodology for the DoD interviews borrowed from the non-DoD interview coding scheme. We first describe the coding methodology for non-DoD interviews and then follow with methodology for the DoD interviews.

Non-DoD Interviews

The coding scheme for the non-DoD leader interviews was adapted from the one used for the job positions. We used the coding schemes developed for the job postings to identify roles and responsibilities and KSAOs in the interviews. However, because the interviews provided richer data, we had to add more codes. In order to capture the breadth of topics covered in the interviews, we developed codes to match each section of the interview protocol. The interview-coding categories include:

- industry
- position title
- position and organizational tenure
- position status (reporting relationships, staff and budget sizes)
- staff roles and responsibilities
- current position's roles and responsibilities
- diversity goals and strategy
- interviewee's assessment of similarity between his or her position and positions held by other diversity leaders
- KSAOs needed for diversity leaders
- previous work experience
- educational and training background (including membership in professional societies)
- definitions of D&I, EEO, and diversity management.

Using the interview-coding scheme, two team members content-coded responses using NVivo software. The two coders independently coded one interview, came together to reconcile coding differences, and then coded another interview to ensure closer agreement in their coding results. Throughout this process, we refined the code descriptions to clarify distinctions between the categories. Once a high level of agreement was reached, the two coders split the remaining interviews and coded most of them independently, conducting a "spot check" along the way to see whether they were still coding in a consistent manner with each other.

Once the coding process was complete, the team's job analysis experts identified themes and connections between interviewees' job roles and responsibilities, professional experiences, educational and training backgrounds, and KSAOs.

DoD Interviews

First, we classified each interview with DoD leaders according to the following characteristics that were unique to the DoD interviewees:

- organization (Army, Coast Guard, etc.)
- leadership level (senior or not-senior).

We used these classifications in our analysis to compare responses across individuals from the different components and between those holding senior and not-senior positions. Given the small sample size, any comparisons across components and leadership level need to be considered carefully. While we cannot assume that one interviewee's response is representative of his or her entire component, the range of responses we observe will still be informative.

Next, one team member coded each response to a question[2] into the following broad categories of interest, based on the types of questions asked:

---

[2]   We had only one team member code these interviews because we had already standardized our coding methodology while coding the non-DoD interviews. This individual was one of two team members who jointly coded the non-DoD interviews. We matched DoD interviewees' responses to our previously defined codes for job responsibilities and KSAOs. Our DoD sample was smaller than our non-DoD sample, and we saw less variation in responses than we did among the non-DoD interviewees. This made the coding process for the DoD interviews more straightforward.

- desired roles and responsibilities for diversity leaders
- KSAOs needed by diversity leaders
- work experience, education, and training needed by diversity leaders
- diversity management office organization and staff requirements.

We also noted responses that distinguished between the job responsibilities and KSAOs needed for diversity leaders compared to EEO/MEO leaders.

After grouping responses into the high-level categories described above, we reviewed the text to identify specific themes. We used the codebook we developed for the non-DoD interviews (the "CDO codebook") to guide this process. However, we also took an exploratory approach and allowed for the possibility that new themes would emerge. Several of the themes related to roles and responsibilities, KSAOs, and experience and training that were defined in the CDO codebook also appeared in the DoD interviews; therefore, we were able to apply the codes that had been previously defined. The range of topics discussed in the DoD interviews was narrower than within the non-DoD interviews, so fewer codes were needed. There were also some nuances in the DoD leaders' responses that were specific to the context of DoD and thus were not apparent in the non-DoD interviews. While we used the same code names and definitions to analyze the DoD interviews, we note any caveats in our discussion.

One area unique to the DoD interviews, and therefore not defined in the CDO codebook, is the topic of how a DoD diversity management office should be structured. After grouping these responses, we coded references to staff roles, personnel mix, and reporting chain arrangements (whether or not diversity leaders should report to senior leaders). See Appendix B for a full description of the codes used to analyze the interviews with DoD leaders.

Job Posting and Interview Coding and Results

This appendix provides the codes used in our content analysis and additional results for the coding analysis of job postings for senior diversity leadership positions and interviews with non-DoD diversity leaders. We do not present detailed results from our DoD interviews because our sample size ($n = 16$) was small and would risk identifying interviewees by inference. However, we provide a section with codes we used that are unique to the DoD interview sample.

Across coding descriptions, we provide tables organized by theme (gray cells) and coding category (first column). Because there can be more than one code per category, we provide a general coding description in the second column.

Job Posting Results

In Tables B.1–B.12, we present the codes and numerical results of our coding analysis of job postings. We counted sources (i.e., job postings) toward the codes; if a posting mentioned the same thing more than once, the posting was only counted once for that code. For example, under the "groups to coordinate, collaborate, and work with" category, statements of "collaborating with faculty" and "working with faculty" in the same posting would only count once toward the "students, faculty, and other academic institution employees (except senior academic leaders)" code. However, one posting can count toward multiple codes in a category: A posting can be coded for both "leadership (academic versus nonacademic)" and "students, faculty, and other academic institution employees (except senior academic leaders)" under the "groups to coordinate, collaborate, and work with" category. Therefore, the results for the codes should be viewed independently (i.e., percentages across codes in a given category will not add up to 100). The two exceptions involve the "industry" and "job title" categories, which have mutually exclusive codes.

Not all job postings contained content that was relevant to each code. We therefore created a code for job postings that did not mention anything relevant to the code. In the results tables, we italicize text in the rows for the "not mentioned" code.

Because the job postings described preferred and required backgrounds and experiences, we delineated between the two in our coding, as reflected by the codes in Tables B.5 and B.7.

Table B.1
Job Postings Codes—Industry and Job Title

Category	Coding Description
Industry	Type of industry for the organization posting the position. Industry types include health care, higher education, media, agriculture and chemicals, and hospitality and tourism.
Job title	Type of position title in the posting. Types of position titles include chief diversity officer, diversity director, and associate/assistant diversity director or dean.

Table B.2
Job Postings Results—Industry and Job Title

Code	% of Postings (n = 53)
Industry	
Higher education	58
Other	17
Health care	13
Media	4
Hospitality and tourism	4
Agriculture and chemicals	4
Job title	
Chief diversity officer	11
Diversity director	42
Associate/assistant diversity dean/vice president/director	21
Diversity program director/ coordinator/manager	13
Diversity adviser/specialist	13

Table B.3
Job Postings Codes—Organizational Relationships

Category	Coding Description
Directly report from	This is who directly reports to the senior diversity leader. This should be coded for associate director or equivalent versus other types of staff.
Directly report to	This is the type of person to which the position reports. This should be coded for senior university leadership (including university presidents, provosts, chancellors, and boards of trustees), corporate executives and boards, and others who fall outside of senior leadership.
Groups to coordinate, collaborate, or work with	These are types of people for which the position requires coordination or collaboration. This should be coded for leadership (academic versus nonacademic); individuals or groups external to the organization; business units; and students, faculty, and other academic institution employees (except senior academic leaders).

Table B.4
Job Postings Results—Organizational Relationships

Codes by Category	% of Postings (*n* = 53)
Directly report from	
Associate director or equivalent	2
Other staff	13
Not mentioned	*85*
Directly report to	
Senior university leadership or board (academia)	38
Senior executives or board (corporate)	23
Program manager	4
Not mentioned	*36*
Groups to coordinate, collaborate, or work with	
Business units/program management staff	60
Students, faculty, or other college employees	45
Individuals/groups outside organization	38
Academic leadership (e.g., deans)	26
Nonacademic leadership (e.g., corporate managers)	26
Not mentioned	*19*

Table B.5
Job Postings Codes—Work Experience

Category	Coding Description
Required experience type	This should be coded if the position specifies a requirement for types of professional work experience (e.g., must have led a diversity program).
Required experience level	This should be coded if the position specifies a required level of professional work experience (e.g., must have five years of leadership experience).
Preferred experience type	This should be coded as for required experience type but focuses on preference for certain types of professional experiences (e.g., prefer someone with previous diversity management position).
Preferred experience level	This should be coded as for required experience level but focuses on preference for certain levels of experience (e.g., prefer five years of leadership experience).
Specific experience type	Types of experience specified in postings, either preferred or required. Types of experience include diversity (e.g., led diversity programs), HR and organizational development (e.g., held an HR position), higher education (e.g., served as faculty), and leadership (e.g., held a management position).

Table B.6
Job Postings Results—Work Experience

Codes by Category	% of Postings ($n = 53$)
Required experience	85
Type	85
Level	62
Preferred experience	60
Type	58
Level	11
Specific experience type	72
Diversity (e.g., led diversity programs)	55
HR and organizational development (e.g., held an HR position)	34
Higher education (e.g., served as faculty)	32
Leadership (e.g., held a management position)	30

Table B.7
Job Postings Codes—Education and Training Background

Category	Coding Description
Required education type	This should be coded if the position specifies any requirement for certain types of education (e.g., must have a bachelor's degree in business).
Required education level	This should be coded as for required education type but for education levels that the position requires (e.g., must have a bachelor's degree).
Preferred education type	This should be coded if the position specifies any preference for certain types of education (e.g., prefer a bachelor's degree in business).
Preferred education level	This should be coded if the position specifies any preference for certain levels of education (e.g., prefer a bachelor's degree).
Required training type	This should be coded as for required education type but focuses on required training (e.g., must have completed training on an EEO topic).
Required training level	This should be coded as for required education level but focuses on required training (e.g., must have completed at least one training course on an EEO topic).
Preferred training type	This should be coded as for preferred education type but focuses on preferred training (e.g., prefer training on an EEO topic).
Preferred training level	This should be coded as for preferred education level but focuses on preferred training (e.g., prefer completion of at least one training course on an EEO topic).
Specific education type/ degree field	Types of education types/degree fields specified in postings, either preferred or required. Types of education include business/organizational development (e.g., masters of business administration), HR, and education.

Table B.8
Job Postings Results—Education and Training Background

Codes by Category	% of Postings (n = 53)
Required education	83
Type	34
Level	60
Preferred education	51
Type	17
Level	34
Required training	2
Type	2
Level	0
Preferred training	2
Type	2
Level	0
Specific education type/ degree field	58
Business/ organizational development	30
HR	25
Education	21
Counseling, psychology, or social work	15
Humanities or social science	11
Law	9
Public health	4
Public administration	2
Physical science or engineering	2

Table B.9
Job Postings Codes—Diversity Leader Roles and Responsibilities

Category	Coding Descriptions
Strategic (diversity) leadership (and management)	
Diversity (and EEO) policies and procedures	Develops, implements, and revises policies and procedures that align with business goals and diversity strategy and may include policies involving EEO compliance. Also includes monitoring policies and procedures to ensure they continue to stay relevant. May provide consultation to leadership on diversity policies.
Diversity programs/initiatives/centers	References to diversity (and multicultural) programs and initiatives (e.g., diversity training for staff, employee resource groups). Includes the development, implementation, and evaluation of programs and initiatives aimed at increasing D&I.
Diversity programs/initiatives/centers subcategory: Lead diversity programs	Denotes a leadership role in diversity programs, initiatives, and centers.
Diversity programs/initiatives/centers subcategory: Support or assist diversity programs	Denotes a supporting role in diversity programs, initiatives, and centers.
Promoting a diverse and inclusive culture	References to promoting a diverse, inclusive, or respectful work environment or culture, without being linked to a specific program or initiative.
Strategic messaging/marketing	(Helps to) develop and implement strategic messages/communication that align with organizational goals. This could include marketing/branding efforts.
Strategic diversity planning and leadership	(Helps to) create and/or implement a strategic vision for D&I. Engages in strategic planning for diversity. Provides leadership/oversight of implementation of strategic diversity plans or initiatives.
EEO activities	
EEO compliance	Ensures that policies, procedures, and practices comply with EEO policy and law (but does not mention actively managing complaints). Includes the creation and oversight of AA plans.
Managing EEO complaints	Manages/officiates EEO complaints (e.g., complaints of harassment or discrimination)

Table B.9—Continued

Category	Coding Descriptions
General management activities	
Budgetary management	Manages operational budget for programs and/or staff. May work with finance departments on larger budgets (e.g., for an entire department).
General project management	References to general tasks related to managing projects, without further specification.
Personnel management	Manages and directs a staff, which can include staff development, performance appraisals, and assigning work tasks.
HR-related activities[a]	
Recruiting, selecting, and retaining diverse talent	Develops and (helps to) implement strategies to attract, select, and retain diverse talent (students, faculty, or other organizational personnel). Activities include advising faculty search committees, and reviewing applicants.
Supporting and retaining students	Supports or advises diverse student groups with the goal of retaining them and ensuring that they graduate.
Tracking diversity trends	
External diversity trends and best practices	Identifies and provides counsel/advice on external trends in diversity (e.g., outside factors likely to affect diversity trends in the organization) and diversity best practices from other organizations.
Internal diversity and EEO metrics	Develops or identifies appropriate diversity-related metrics or outcome metrics for diversity programs and initiatives. May also engage in tracking or monitoring and conducting analysis to identify trends or managing personnel who monitor and analyze metrics. Often followed by reporting on trends and outcomes to organizational leaders and/or organizational community (e.g., campus students, faculty, and staff). Includes any reference to evaluating or assessing a program or initiative. (This may be double-coded with "diversity programs/initiatives/centers.")
Stakeholder engagement	
Advising/counseling leaders on diversity	Advises or counsels organizational leaders (e.g., university president) on diversity and EEO issues.
Advising/counseling students on diversity	Advises or counsels students or student groups as part of diversity programs or efforts. Does not include academic advising (see "supporting and retaining students").

Table B.9—Continued

Category	Coding Descriptions
External engagement	Represents organization to outside community, clients, or other external stakeholders in matters related to diversity and multicultural affairs. May involve developing organization-community partnerships or connections through activities (e.g., conferences) to improve organizational-community relationships. (For example, a company might want to partner with universities with diverse pools of students.)
Educate internal stakeholders on diversity	Educates faculty, staff, and other personnel in the organization about diversity initiatives, metrics, and general diversity-related issues. Provides consultation, advising, or guidance or serves as a resource for staff and internal groups regarding diversity. (This is separate from counseling or advising students as part of diversity programs and separate from diversity-related training for staff.) Promotes a diverse, inclusive, and respectful work environment. (This may be double-coded with diversity programs and initiatives.)

[a] Though it was not included for the job postings, this category also included a "supplier diversity" code for our interviews.

Table B.10
Job Postings Results—Diversity Leader Roles and Responsibilities

Codes by Category	% of Postings ($n = 53$)
Strategic (diversity) leadership (and management)[a]	100
Diversity programs/initiatives/centers	92
Lead diversity programs	83
Support or assist diversity programs	38
Strategic diversity planning and leadership	72
Diversity (and EEO) policies and procedures	38
Promoting a diverse and inclusive culture	32
Strategic messaging/marketing	26
Stakeholder engagement	83
External engagement	62

Table B.10—Continued

Codes by Category	% of Postings (*n* = 53)
Advising/counseling leaders on diversity	42
Educating internal stakeholders on diversity	38
Advising/counseling students on diversity	9
Tracking diversity trends	64
Internal diversity and EEO metrics	60
External diversity trends and best practices	38
HR-related activities[b]	60
Recruiting, selecting, and retaining diverse talent	49
Supporting and retaining students	23
General management activities	36
Personnel management	32
Budgetary management	13
General project management	8
EEO activities	28
EEO compliance	26
Managing EEO complaints	13

[a] Not all job postings reflected senior-level diversity jobs, so not all percentages in the leadership category are at the strategic level.

[b] Though it was not included for the job postings, this category also included a "supplier diversity" code for our interviews.

Table B.11
Job Postings Codes—KSAOs

Category	Coding Descriptions
Analytical abilities and skills	
Skills involving data and metrics	References to analytical ability or skills (e.g., analysis, research, and interpreting data or information).
EEO, AA, and diversity knowledge and skills	
Commitment to diversity[a]	Descriptions of interest, commitment, or even passion for diversity, inclusion, and other fairness or social justice issues (e.g., equity). Also includes references to being an advocate for those issues.
Compliance and legislation	References to knowledge and/or experience working in the areas of EO, civil rights, and AA legislation and policies.
Diversity and cultural program experience	Work experience with diversity and/or cultural programs and initiatives. References to diversity management/ leadership or having a diversity background.
Knowledge of D&I issues	References to general "diversity and inclusion" knowledge. This is separate from knowledge of compliance legislation.
Interpersonal skills (and experience)[b]	
Collaboration/ teamwork skills and experience	Descriptions of interacting with others that involve collaboration or teamwork. Also includes references to working well with others. Includes interactions, networking, or relationship-building with internal stakeholders. Excludes networking with external stakeholders.
Communication skills and experience	Skill and experience communicating (verbally or in writing) to multiple audiences (e.g., facilitation, presentation, explaining complex problems). This also includes descriptions referring to active listening or facilitating meetings with clients.
Consulting skills and experience	References to consulting skills or experience as a consultant.
Counseling, mediation, and conflict resolution	References to skills or experience related to conflict resolution, mediation, or counseling. Includes conflict resolution or mediation with different racial or ethnic groups. Includes references to "team interventions" and negotiation.
General interpersonal skills	References to general interpersonal skills without further specification. May include general interactions with clients.

Table B.11—Continued

Category	Coding Descriptions
Influence/persuasion skills and experience	Descriptions of influencing or persuading others. Includes negotiation and consensus-building.
Intercultural interaction skills and experience	Descriptions of experience or skill at interacting with people from different racial or ethnic cultures. Includes general experience working in a diverse or multicultural environment or managing diverse teams. Also includes references to having intercultural competencies, being sensitive and respectful to different cultures, and possessing ability to build trust. (This is a subset of general interpersonal skills and experience, so it can include collaboration, negotiation, influence, and persuasion.)
Mentoring/developing people	References to a willingness or desire to mentor or professionally develop others. Includes mentoring and advising experience.
Networking with external stakeholders	References to skill or experience related to networking or relationship-building with external organizations or stakeholders. Includes references to public relations or interacting with customers.

Leadership skills (and experience)

Category	Coding Descriptions
General management/ leadership skills and experience	References to management or leadership experience and skills in general (e.g., leading and motivating subordinates, delegating responsibilities, supervising others or work tasks, etc.) or in reference to developing, running, and/or assessing programs.
Organizational improvement/change	References to experience or skill at fostering, creating, or improving the organizational environment to make it inclusive or innovative. Also includes references to "change" leadership or management and organizational development.
Project management skills and experience	Descriptions of having skill or experience in managing projects, including managing resources (budgets, operations, and people) and being able to meet deadlines.
Strategic leadership skills and experience	References to experience or skill in developing strategy or using "strategic thinking." Includes such things as creating and implementing a vision and developing strategic plans and initiatives.

Personality and attitude[a,c]

Category	Coding Descriptions
Adaptability	Descriptions of "navigating" or reacting well to novel or complex situations or settings, handling change or adversity, being flexible, and being open to feedback or criticism.

Table B.11—Continued

Category	Coding Descriptions
Driven/motivated	References to having initiative; being a "self-starter"; or being driven, proactive, goal-oriented, or motivated. Also includes persistence under adversity, patience, having a strong work ethic, and having a positive attitude.
Integrity	References to having integrity, having good judgment, and/or being ethical or fair.
Organizational skills (Conscientiousness)	References to being organized, detail-oriented, or planful. This also includes references to time management and prioritizing activities, as well as the ability to multitask.
Personable	References to being personable, easy to interact with, friendly, or "nice."
Resourceful	Descriptions of being resourceful, practical, or capable.
Responsible	Descriptions of being responsible, dependable, or reliable. Setting and meeting goals and personal accountability.
Other personality traits	Includes references that do not fit in the other personality categories (e.g., forward-thinking).
Technical skills or experience[d]	
Business technical skills	Descriptions of understanding and/or applying business principles, techniques, etc. Includes financial skills and experience.
Computer skills	References to knowing how to use Microsoft Office software or other general information technology and business software.
Human resources[d]	References to knowledge and/or application of HR programs, processes, and systems. This includes references to "human capital," "talent" management, or recruitment.
Training experience	Experience in developing, implementing, and/or evaluating training programs.
Other KSAOs	
Confidentiality	References to being able to keep sensitive information confidential.
Independence	References to working independently.

Table B.11—Continued

Category	Coding Descriptions
Miscellaneous KSAOs	Includes references that do not fit in the other KSA categories. References to meeting client needs, fundraising, etc.

[a] Although we originally coded "commitment to diversity" as part of the category of "EEO, AA, and diversity knowledge and skills," we discuss it in the context of "personality and attitude" because it reflects an attitude, not a knowledge or skill area.

[b] Though it was not included for the job postings, this category also included a "political savvy" code for our interviews.

[c] Though it was not included for the job postings, this category also included an "empathy" code for our interviews.

[d] For our interviews, we separated business expertise and technical skills. This distinction was not necessary for the job postings, which focus on technical skills. Human resources is included under "technical skills or experience" for job postings and is included under "business expertise" for the interviews.

Table B.12
Job Postings Results—KSAOs

Codes by Category	% of Postings (*n* = 53)
Interpersonal skills (and experience)[a]	92
Communication skills and experience	81
General interpersonal skills	70
Collaboration/teamwork skills and experience	70
Intercultural interaction skills and experience	43
Networking with external stakeholders	42
Influence/persuasion skills and experience	23
Mentoring/developing people	23
Counseling, mediation, and conflict resolution	15
Consulting skills and experience	4
EEO, AA, and diversity knowledge and skills	92
Diversity and cultural program experience	68
Knowledge of D&I issues	34
Compliance and legislation	32
Commitment to diversity[b]	30
Leadership skills (and experience)	87
General management/leadership skills and experience	55
Project management skills and experience	55
Strategic leadership skills and experience	40
Organizational improvement/change	32
Personality and attitude[b, c]	72
Organizational skills (conscientiousness)	43
Driven/motivated	42
Integrity	28

Table B.12—Continued

Codes by Category	% of Postings ($n = 53$)
Adaptability	19
Responsible	19
Resourceful	9
Personable	6
Other personality traits	6
Technical skills or experience[d]	68
Human resources[d]	36
Computer skills	30
Training experience	25
Business technical skills	21
Analytical abilities and skills	43
Skills involving data and metrics	43
Other KSAOs	30
Confidentiality	23
Independence	17
Miscellaneous KSAOs	19

[a] Though it was not included for the job postings, this category also included a "political savvy" code for our interviews

[b] Although we originally coded "commitment to diversity" as part of the category of "EEO, AA, and diversity knowledge and skills," we discuss it in the context of "personality and attitude" because it reflects an attitude, not a knowledge or skill area.

[c] Though it was not included for the job postings, this category also included an "empathy" code for our interviews.

[d] For our interviews, we separated business expertise and technical skills. This distinction was not necessary for the job postings, which focus on technical skills. Human resources is included under "technical skills or experience" for job postings and is included under "business expertise" for the interviews.

Non-DoD Interview Codes and Results

Tables B.13–B.32 provide codes and numerical results from the content analysis of non-DoD diversity leadership interviews. We interviewed 47 individuals, but two of the 47 were not in senior leadership positions. We therefore removed them from analyses that directly tie to diversity leadership positions, such as their reporting chain and roles and responsibilities. We retained them for analysis of KSAOs because we asked about KSAOs needed by diversity leaders in general. In the following tables, if the sample size, n, equals 47, all participants were included in analysis. If n equals 45, the two participants were removed from the analysis.

In most cases, the codes are straightforward or generally follow the coding definitions used for job postings. We therefore do not include separate coding tables for many coding categories, specifically the categories that relate to interviewee background (e.g., organization tenure, position tenure) or the basic structure of their positions (e.g., reporting chain). Instead, we provide context about the coding in the notes section underneath the appropriate results tables. See, for example, notes associated with Tables B.13–B.16.

Table B.13
Non-DoD Interview Results—Industry and Job Title

Codes by Category	% of Interviews ($n = 47$)
Organization type	
For-profit (corporate)	55
Federal government	28
Higher education	13
Local government	2
Unassigned (other not-for-profit)	2
Title	
CDO	68
Other	11
Associate/assistant diversity dean/vice president	9
EEO director	6
Diversity director	4
Diversity program director/manager	2

NOTES: "Industry" refers to type of organization and includes higher education, corporate or for-profit, federal government, and local government. All of the organization types besides for-profit (corporate) can be classified as not-for-profit, as they are in our supplementary analyses in Chapters Two and Three. "Job Title" refers to the interviewee's current position title. Those categorized as "other" had a variety of position titles that did not clearly fit into existing categories.

Table B.14
Non-DoD Interview Results—
Position Tenure

Code	% of Interviews ($n = 47$)
Years in current position	
Less than 1 year	9
1 to 5 years	68
6 to 10 years	15
More than 10 years	9

NOTES: We asked participants how long they had been in their current positions. To code position tenure, we grouped the years into intervals, as shown in the table. We chose to split out those who had less than a year in their positions from those with more than a year to determine how much experience an interviewee had in a given position.

Table B.15
Non-DoD Interview Results—
Organization Tenure

Code	% of Interviews ($n = 45$)
Amount of career spent in the organization	
Joined recently	16
Some of career	22
Most of career	18
Entire career	7
Unknown	38

NOTES: We did not specifically ask participants about organization tenure. Many interviewees did not specify the number of years spent in their current organization. Instead, many used qualitative statements. We used those statements to get a sense of organization tenure. Interviewees who did not specify any organization tenure are coded as "unknown."

Table B.16
Non-DoD Interview Results—
Reporting Chain

Code	% of Interviews ($n = 45$)
Vice president or head of HR	40
Head of organization (e.g., chief executive officer, president)	27
Other	33

NOTES: We asked participants to identify to whom they directly reported. Most participants stated that they reported directly to a vice president or to a top organization leader (chief executive officer, president). The "other" category includes such senior leadership positions as chief financial officer, chief operating officer, general counsel, chief administrative officer, and chief academic officer.

Table B.17
Non-DoD Interview Codes—Office Structure

Category	Coding Description
No function	Does not oversee a function or office, department, or unit.
Diversity	Only oversees a diversity function.
EEO	Only oversees EEO/AA/civil rights functions.
Diversity and EEO	Oversees diversity function as well as EEO/AA/civil rights function. May also have other functions not specifically related to diversity or EEO, such as HR.
Diversity and other	Oversees diversity function as well as other functions not specifically related to diversity, but does not have EEO/AA/civil rights as part of his or her function.
EEO and other	Oversees EEO/AA/civil rights as one part of his or her function, in addition to other non–diversity-related functions, such as HR functions.

Table B.18
Non-DoD Interview Results—Office
Structure, Staff, and Budget

Codes by Category	% of Interviews ($n = 45$)
Primary responsibility areas of department/office	
Diversity and EEO	38
Diversity	36
Diversity and other	22
EEO	2
EEO and other	2
Size of diversity office staff	
None	4
Less than 10	33
10–20	18
21–40	0
40 or more	4
No answer[a]	40
Budget	
Yes	82
No	2
No answer	16

NOTES: In addition to asking participants about their primary areas of responsibility, we asked them how many individuals they have on staff doing diversity work and whether they have their own operating budgets.

[a] The "no answer" code for diversity office staff size includes individuals without diversity office staff (e.g., those with only EEO responsibilities), as well as some individuals who declined to answer the question.

Table B.19
Non-DoD Interview Codes—Prior Work Experience

Category	Coding Description
Human resources	Previous jobs include various HR-related positions (e.g., recruiting, outreach, compensation, organizational development).
Law	Previous job as a lawyer; if this is related to compliance or EEO laws, we double-coded with the EEO category.
Business	References to previous jobs held in general business-type positions (e.g., operations, strategy, finance, accounting) or something for which one may need a business degree. Excludes marketing experience.
Consulting	References to working as a consultant, either diversity consulting or general organizational consulting. Also included if the interviewee mentioned having worked at a consulting firm, even if specific job title or function is not provided.
Academia	Mentions working or teaching in a university setting.
Communications/ marketing	References previous positions focused on marketing or strategic communications.
Other	References to other types of work experience.
EEO position	Was at one point in a position that focused on compliance, EEO, or AA.
Diversity position	Was at one point in a position that focused on D&I; this could include other CDO positions or lower-level diversity-related positions; this does not include EEO-focused positions.
Military diversity experience	References to having had diversity- or MEO-related positions in the military; served on active duty or as reservist or guardsman. Excludes positions as a civilian working for DoD or the military.

**Table B.20
Non-DoD Interview Results—
Prior Work Experience**

Codes by Category	% of Interviews ($n = 45$)
Diversity position	60
Human resources	51
Business	49
Other	47
EEO position	27
Communications/ marketing	20
Academia	18
Consulting	13
Law	13
Military diversity experience	11

NOTES: We used the job posting categories of types of work experience as a baseline for coding prior work experience of non-DoD diversity leaders. However, we expanded to include areas such as "military diversity experience."

Table B.21
Non-DoD Interview Codes—Education and Training Background

Category	Coding Description
Highest degree earned	Bachelor's, master's, Ph.D., or J.D.
Degree subject area	HR/organizational development, business, law, communications, or other area.
Other training and education	
Diversity training or education	Yes or no, has or has not taken specific courses or training programs related to diversity.
Conferences	Describes learning and education occurring through attendance at various conferences, in general.
Leadership training	Mentions taking general leadership courses, which may or may not be related specifically to diversity.
EEO-related	Mentions courses specifically focused on EEO, compliance, and/or AA.
Mediation	Mentions courses specifically focused on mediation.
Specific courses or conferences for "other" training/education	
Specific diversity education programs	Mentions the Cornell or Georgetown diversity management programs. Most mention in the context of programs to which they have sent their staff or have heard about but not attended.
Specific classes or conferences	Any references to attending classes or conferences run by the following organizations: Conference Board, DEOMI, Multicultural Forum, Linkage, Catalyst, Working Mother Media, SHRM, Diversity Best Practices, or other organization. Most participants have attended these conferences at some point in their careers.

Table B.22
Non-DoD Interview Results—Education and
Training Background

Codes by Category	% of Interviews ($n = 45$)
Highest degree earned	
No college degree	2
Bachelor's degree	31
Master's degree	40
J.D.	11
Ph.D.	13
Unknown (did not specify)	2
Degree subject area	
HR/organizational development	24
Business	18
Communications	16
Law	16
Other[a]	56
Other training and education	
Diversity training or education	69
Conferences	67
Leadership training	27
EEO courses	18
Mediation courses	11
Specific courses or conferences for "other" training/education	
Conference Board	42
Cornell program	22
SHRM	18
Diversity Best Practices	18
Catalyst	16
DEOMI courses	11

Table B.22—Continued

Codes by Category	% of Interviews (*n* = 45)
Working Mother Media	11
Linkage	9
Multicultural Forum	7
Georgetown program	4
Other[a]	87

[a] The "other" codes for degree subject area and specific courses or conferences cover the degree subject areas and courses or conferences that were identified by fewer than five participants.

Table B.23
Non-DoD Interview Codes—Diversity Strategy and Goals

Category	Coding Description
Status of diversity strategy/plan	Indicates whether the organization does not have a strategy/plan, is working on a strategy/plan, or has a strategy/plan.
Diversity goals or strategic pillars	
Enhance marketplace presence	Denotes D&I strategies to enhance the organization's market presence (e.g., enter new markets), make a reputation for diversity in the external community, better assist customers and clients, work with diverse suppliers, etc.
Ensure EO/AA for all	Describes an EEO/AA focus for a goal (e.g., ensuring that everyone has equal access and opportunity to reach full potential).
Increase workforce diversity	Describes a goal or mission to develop and implement strategies to recruit, select, develop, and/or retain qualified individuals from various groups (e.g., segments of American society, global cultural groups) in order to build a diverse workforce that meets the organization's mission needs. May also mention trying to develop diverse leadership in the organization.
Foster an inclusive culture in organization and engage employees	Indicates a goal or mission to develop a culture of inclusion and engagement in the organization so that individuals can meet their full potential.
Sustain D&I commitment in organization	Describes institutionalizing or sustaining D&I strategies and efforts through alignment of D&I strategies with business goals and through continued leadership commitment, involvement, and accountability for D&I.
Other goal	Description of other goals or strategic pillars for diversity.

Table B.24
Non-DoD Interview Results—
Diversity Strategy and Goals

Codes by Category	% of Interviews (n = 47)
Status of diversity strategy/plan	
Yes, has strategy/plan	72
In progress	9
No strategy/plan	0
Unknown or unclear	21
Diversity goals or strategic pillars	
Foster an inclusive culture in organization and engage employees	60
Sustain D&I commitment in organization	53
Increase workforce diversity	49
Enhance marketplace presence	40
Ensure EO/AA for all	17
Other	17

NOTES: We asked participants whether their organizations had diversity strategies or plans. The codes follow a yes/no pattern except in cases in which participants said that the plan/strategy was in progress or was being developed or modified. Twenty-one participants did not (clearly) indicate whether their organizations had diversity strategies or plans.

Table B.25
Non-DoD Interview Codes—Definitions of Diversity, EEO, and Related Terms

Category	Coding Descriptions
Diversity definition	
Characteristics/differences	Defines diversity as differences (and similarities) between people. Might specify some EEO protected categories (e.g., race/ethnicity, gender) but does not restrict description to just protected categories.
Fairness/equal opportunity	Describes diversity in terms of making sure everyone is treated fairly and has opportunities.
Organizational opportunity or imperative	Describes diversity as opportunity for organizations. Might mention the context of changing U.S. demographics.
Organizational imperative subcategory: Representation	States that workforce and/or leadership of the organization should reflect the diversity of the nation.
Organizational imperative subcategory: External stakeholders	States that diversity is needed to tap into a diverse client base or to work with other external stakeholders (e.g., community groups).
Miscellaneous diversity definitions	Offers another definition of diversity not listed above.
Inclusion definition	
Leveraging diversity	Describes inclusion as leveraging diversity for meeting business or organizational goals.
Employee engagement	Inclusion involves engaging employees. Might mention inclusive climate, climate of engagement, or making sure all voices are heard.
Fairness	Inclusion described as fairness or fair treatment of people. Fairness may be related to EO.
Miscellaneous inclusion definitions	Offers another definition of inclusion not listed above.
EEO definition	
Foundation for diversity	Indicates that EEO provides the foundation for diversity (and inclusion).
Compliance/legal	Defines EEO as a legal obligation, having to do with compliance.

Table B.25—Continued

Category	Coding Descriptions
Representation	Defines EEO as workforce representation in terms of protected groups.
Fairness/creating opportunity	Defines EEO as fair practices, making sure that people have opportunities.
Should be separate from diversity	Indicates that EEO should not be part of diversity or is outdated (should be left behind).
Miscellaneous EEO definitions	Offers another definition of EEO not listed above.
Diversity management definition	
Processes/practices for diversity	Defines diversity management as processes and/ or practices to carry out diversity plans and goals. Examples include how the organization targets diverse talent for recruitment, processes for ensuring a diverse pool of candidates for promotion, and practices around goals for supplier diversity, etc.
Akin to general leadership	Defines diversity management as being a good leader or manager.
Engaging workforce	Defines diversity management as leadership behaviors aimed at engaging a diverse workforce.
Does not use term	Indicates that he or she does not use the term "diversity management." Sees it as negative or outdated.
Miscellaneous diversity management definitions	Offers another definition of diversity management not listed above.

Table B.26
Non-DoD Interview Results—
Definitions of Diversity, EEO, and Related Terms

Codes by Category	% of Interviews (n = 45)
Diversity	94
Characteristics/differences	79
Miscellaneous diversity definitions	17
Fairness/equal opportunity	15
Organizational opportunity or imperative	4
Organizational imperative: Representation	6
Organizational imperative subcategory: External stakeholders	4
Inclusion	87
Employee engagement	51
Leveraging diversity	32
Miscellaneous inclusion definitions	21
Fairness	19
Diversity management	96
Processes/practices for diversity	40
Engaging workforce	32
Does not use this term	21
Miscellaneous diversity management definitions	19
Akin to general leadership	9
EEO	77
Compliance/legal	40
Foundation for diversity	36
Fairness/creating opportunity	13
Should be separate from diversity	13
Miscellaneous EEO definitions	4
Representation	4

Table B.27
Non-DoD Interview Codes—Staff Roles and Responsibilities

Category	Coding Description
Administrative activities	Provides administrative support to the CDO and/or CDO staff. Activities include managing the CDO's schedule, helping with logistics for events, etc.
EEO activities subcategory: EEO compliance or complaints	Denotes responsibility for EEO functions. Activities may include managing/officiating EEO complaints (e.g., complaints of harassment or discrimination).
EEO activities subcategory: AA	Denotes responsibility for AA functions. May include developing AA plans or managing AA programs.
Diversity programs/ initiatives/centers	Denotes a role in diversity programs, initiatives, and centers. Includes day-to-day operations, budget management, and other program management activities. Includes employee resource groups and diversity councils.
Stakeholder engagement subcategory: External stakeholder engagement	Develops relationships with external community, including industry groups and racial/ethnic communities. For example, (helps to) run conferences or other external events. (May be double-coded with "diversity programs/initiatives/centers.")
Stakeholder engagement subcategory: Supplier diversity	Works with vendors and other external clients to identify opportunities for a diverse client base. May also focus on diversifying amongst vendors. (This is a type of external stakeholder engagement but with a specific focus on suppliers.)
Training and education	Develops and provides training on diversity and/or EEO matters to personnel in the organization. (This is separate from coordinating or facilitating training courses or programs.)
Tracking diversity trends	Tracking and monitoring metrics and conducting analyses to identify trends for diversity and/or EEO. May help develop reports on trends and outcomes that the CDO will share with organizational leaders and/or the organizational community (e.g., campus students, faculty, and staff). Includes any reference to evaluating or assessing a program or initiative, including helping to develop and evaluate employee surveys. May include benchmarking in the organization's industry.
HR-related activities	Helps to implement strategies to attract, select, and retain diverse talent (students, faculty, or other organizational personnel). Activities include advising faculty search committees, reviewing applicants, and partnering with HR departments for outreach and recruiting activities.

Table B.27—Continued

Category	Coding Description
Communication	Works with the CDO to develop and implement diversity-related messages and communication that align with organizational goals (e.g., has oversight of diversity messaging on external website).
Miscellaneous job responsibilities	Includes references that do not fit in the other staff job responsibilities categories.

NOTE: Only EEO activities and stakeholder engagement have subcodes.

Table B.28
Non-DoD Interview Results—
Staff Roles and Responsibilities

Codes by Category	% of Interviews ($n = 47$)
Diversity programs/initiatives/centers	68
Training and education	60
Tracking diversity trends	55
Stakeholder engagement	43
External stakeholder engagement	40
Supplier diversity	9
Communication	36
EEO activities	36
EEO compliance or complaints	30
AA	15
Miscellaneous job responsibilities	30
Administrative activities	26
HR-related activities	21

Table B.29
Non-DoD Interview Codes—Diversity Leader Roles and Responsibilities

Category	Coding Descriptions
Strategic (diversity) leadership (and management)	
Diversity (and EEO) policies and procedures	Develops, implements, and revises policies and procedures that align with business goals and diversity strategy, and may include policies involving EEO compliance. Also includes monitoring policies and procedures to ensure they continue to stay relevant. May provide consultation to leadership on diversity policies.
Diversity programs/ initiatives/centers	References to diversity (and multicultural) programs and initiatives (e.g., diversity training for staff, employee resource groups). Includes the development, implementation, and evaluation of programs and initiatives aimed at increasing D&I.
Diversity programs/ initiatives/centers subcategory: Lead diversity programs	Denotes a leadership role in diversity programs, initiatives, and centers.
Diversity programs/ initiatives/centers subcategory: Support or assist diversity programs	Denotes a supporting role in diversity programs, initiatives, and centers.
Promoting a diverse and inclusive culture	References to promoting a diverse, inclusive, or respectful work environment or culture, without being linked to a specific program or initiative.
Strategic messaging/ marketing	(Helps to) develop and implement strategic messages/ communication that align with organizational goals. This could include marketing/branding efforts.
Strategic diversity planning and leadership	(Helps to) create and/or implement a strategic vision for D&I. Engages in strategic planning for diversity. Provides leadership/oversight of implementation of strategic diversity plans or initiatives.
EEO activities	
EEO compliance	Ensures policies, procedures, and practices comply with EEO policy and law (but does not mention actively managing complaints). Includes the creation and oversight of AA plans.
Managing EEO complaints	Manages/officiates EEO complaints (e.g., complaints of harassment or discrimination).

Table B.29—Continued

Category	Coding Descriptions
General management activities[a]	
Budgetary management	Manages operational budget for programs and/or staff. May work with finance departments on larger budgets (e.g., for an entire department).
Personnel management	Manages and directs a staff, which can include staff development, performance appraisals, and assigning work tasks.
HR-related activities[b]	
Recruiting, selecting, and retaining diverse talent	Develops and (helps to) implement strategies to attract, select, and retain diverse talent (students, faculty, or other organizational personnel). Activities include advising faculty search committees and reviewing applicants.
Supplier diversity	Ensures that vendors and suppliers to the organization are diverse.
Tracking diversity trends	
External diversity trends and best practices	Identifies and provides counsel/advice on external trends in diversity (e.g., outside factors likely to affect diversity trends in the organization) and diversity best practices from other organizations.
Internal diversity and EEO metrics	Develops or identifies appropriate diversity-related metrics or outcome metrics for diversity programs and initiatives. May also engage in tracking or monitoring and conducting analysis to identify trends, or managing personnel who monitor and analyze metrics. Often followed by reporting on trends and outcomes to organizational leaders and/or organizational community (e.g., campus students, faculty, and staff). Includes any reference to evaluating or assessing a program or initiative. (May be double-coded with "diversity programs/initiatives/centers.")
Stakeholder engagement	
Advising/counseling leaders on diversity	Advises or counsels organizational leaders (e.g., university president) on diversity and EEO issues.
Advising/counseling students on diversity	Advises or counsels students or student groups as part of diversity programs or efforts. Does not include academic advising.

Table B.29—Continued

Category	Coding Descriptions
External engagement	Represents organization to outside community, clients, or other external stakeholders in matters related to diversity and multicultural affairs. May involve developing organization-community partnerships or connections through activities (e.g., conferences) to improve organizational-community relationships. (For example, a company might want to partner with universities with diverse pools of students.)
Educate internal stakeholders on diversity	Educates faculty, staff, and other personnel in the organization about diversity initiatives, metrics, and general diversity-related issues. Provides consultation, advising, or guidance or serves as a resource for staff and internal groups regarding diversity. (This is separate from counseling or advising students as part of diversity programs and separate from diversity-related training for staff.) Promotes a diverse, inclusive, and respectful work environment. (This may be double-coded with "diversity programs/initiatives/centers.")

NOTES: The codes in this table are largely the same as those in Table B.9. We present the codes again to aid readers in their interpretation of the results in Table B.30.

[a] Though it was not included for our interviews, this category also included a "general project management" code for the job postings.

[b] Though it was not included for our interviews, this category also included a "supporting and retaining students" code for the job postings.

**Table B.30
Non-DoD Interview Results—
Diversity Leader Roles and Responsibilities**

Codes by Category	% of Interviews ($n = 45$)
Strategic (diversity) leadership (and management)	100
Strategic diversity planning and leadership	87
Diversity programs/initiatives/centers	82
Lead diversity programs	18
Support or assist diversity programs	9
Promoting a diverse and inclusive culture	42
Strategic messaging/marketing	38
Diversity (and EEO) policies and procedures	9
Stakeholder engagement	100
Advising/counseling leaders on diversity	96
Educate internal stakeholders on diversity	78
External engagement	73
Advising/counseling students on diversity	9
Tracking diversity trends	84
Internal diversity and EEO metrics	73
External diversity trends and best practices	36
HR-related activities[a]	73
Recruiting, selecting, and retaining diverse talent	73
Supplier diversity	9
General management activities[b]	38
Personnel management	33
Budgetary management	11
EEO activities	33
EEO compliance	29
Managing EEO complaints	9

[a] Though it was not included for our interviews, this category also included a "supporting and retaining students" code for the job postings.

[b] Though it was not included for our interviews, this category also included a "general project management" code for the job postings.

Table B.31
Non-DoD Interview Codes—KSAOs

Category	Coding Descriptions
Analytical abilities and skills	
Skills involving data and metrics	References to analytical ability or skills (e.g., analysis, research, and interpreting data or information).
EEO, AA, and diversity knowledge and skills	
Commitment to diversity[a]	Descriptions of interest, commitment, or even passion for diversity, inclusion, and other fairness or social justice issues (e.g., equity). Also includes references to being an advocate for those issues.
Compliance and legislation	References to knowledge and/or experience working in the areas of EO, civil rights, and AA legislation and policies.
Diversity and cultural program experience	Work experience with diversity and/or cultural programs and initiatives. References to diversity management/leadership or having a diversity background.
Knowledge of D&I issues	References to general "diversity and inclusion" knowledge. This is separate from knowledge of compliance legislation.
Interpersonal skills (and experience)	
Collaboration/teamwork skills and experience	Descriptions of interacting with others that involve collaboration or teamwork. Also includes references to working well with others. Includes interactions, networking, or relationship-building with internal stakeholders. Excludes networking with external stakeholders.
Communication skills and experience	Skill and experience communicating (verbally or in writing) to multiple audiences (e.g., facilitation, presentation, explaining complex problems). This also includes descriptions referring to active listening or facilitating meetings with clients.
Consulting skills and experience	References to consulting skills or experience as a consultant.
Counseling, mediation, and conflict resolution	References to skills or experience related to conflict resolution, mediation, or counseling. Includes conflict resolution or mediation with different racial or ethnic groups. Includes references to "team interventions" and negotiation.

Table B.31—Continued

Category	Coding Descriptions
General interpersonal skills	References to general interpersonal skills without further specification. May include general interactions with clients.
Influence/persuasion skills and experience	Descriptions of influencing or persuading others. Includes negotiation and consensus-building.
Intercultural interaction skills and experience	Descriptions of experience or skill at interacting with people from different racial or ethnic cultures. Includes general experience working in a diverse or multicultural environment or managing diverse teams. Also includes references to having intercultural competencies, being sensitive and respectful to different cultures, and possessing ability to build trust. (This is a subset of general interpersonal skills and experience, so it can include collaboration, negotiation, influence, and persuasion.)
Mentoring/developing people	References to a willingness or desire to mentor or professionally develop others. Includes mentoring and advising experience.
Networking with external stakeholders	References to skill or experience related to networking or relationship-building with external organizations or stakeholders. Includes references to public relations or interacting with customers.
Political savvy	Having political knowledge or skills. Understanding who the key players in the organization are and how to build relationships with them to "get things done." Involves the ability to navigate sensitive matters in a way that does not "burn bridges" but instead maximizes benefits for all those involved. Includes having knowledge about specific individuals and what they can offer.
Leadership skills (and experience)	
General management/ leadership skills and experience	References to management or leadership experience and skills in general (e.g., leading and motivating subordinates, delegating responsibilities, supervising others or work tasks, etc.) or in reference to developing, running, and/or assessing programs.
Organizational improvement/change	References to experience or skill at fostering, creating, or improving the organizational environment to make it inclusive or innovative. Also includes references to "change" leadership or management and organizational development.

Table B.31—Continued

Category	Coding Descriptions
Project management skills and experience	Descriptions of having skill or experience in managing projects, including managing resources (budgets, operations, and people) and being able to meet deadlines.
Strategic leadership skills and experience	References to experience or skill in developing strategy or using "strategic thinking." Includes such things as creating and implementing a vision and developing strategic plans and initiatives.
Personality and attitude[a, b]	
Adaptability	Descriptions of "navigating" or reacting well to novel or complex situations or settings, handling change or adversity, being flexible, and being open to feedback or criticism.
Driven/motivated	References to having initiative; being a "self-starter"; or being driven, proactive, goal-oriented, or motivated. Also includes persistence under adversity, patience, having a strong work ethic, and having a positive attitude.
Empathy	References to being empathetic or able to relate to and acknowledge others' feelings and perspectives. Includes references to having "emotional IQ" or "emotional intelligence."
Integrity	References to having integrity, good judgment, and/or being ethical or fair.
Organizational skills (Conscientiousness)	References to being organized, detail-oriented, or planful. This also includes references to time management and prioritizing activities, as well as the ability to multitask.
Personable	References to being personable, easy to interact with, friendly, or "nice."
Resourceful	Descriptions of being resourceful, practical, or capable.
Other personality traits	Includes references that do not fit in the other personality categories (e.g., forward-thinking).
Business expertise[c]	
Expertise on external business environment	An understanding of the current business climate (competitors, market, etc.) and the needs of different client and customer bases. The ability to track external trends and apply lessons to one's own organizational context.

Table B.31—Continued

Category	Coding Descriptions
Intraorganizational expertise	Understanding the "business," or the organization's operations and goals. Refers to knowing how to link D&I strategies to those core business operations and how to talk to business unit leaders in their "language."
Human resources[c]	References to knowledge and/or application of HR programs, processes, and systems. This includes references to "human capital," "talent" management, or recruitment.
Technical skills or experience	
Computer skills	References to knowing how to use Microsoft Office software or other general information technology and business software.
Training experience	Experience in developing, implementing, and/or evaluating training programs.
Miscellaneous KSAOs[d]	Includes references that do not fit in the other KSAO categories. References to meeting client needs, fundraising, etc.

NOTES: The codes in this table are largely the same as those in Table B.11. We present the codes again to aid readers in their interpretation of the results in Table B.32.

[a] Although we originally coded "commitment to diversity" as part of the category of "EEO, AA, and diversity knowledge and skills," we discuss it in the context of "personality and attitude" because it reflects an attitude, not a knowledge or skill area.

[b] Though it was not included for our interviews, this category also included a "responsible" code for the job postings.

[c] For our interviews, we separated business expertise and technical skills. This distinction was not necessary for the job postings, which focus on technical skills. Human resources is under "technical skills or experience" for job postings and is included under "business expertise" for the interviews.

[d] Though they were not included for our interviews, this table also included an "Other KSAOs" category that contained "confidentiality" and "independence" codes for the job postings.

Table B.32
Non-DoD Interview Results—KSAOs

Codes by Category	% of Interviews (n = 47)
Interpersonal skills (and experience)	94
Communication skills and experience	72
Influence/persuasion skills and experience	49
Collaboration/teamwork skills and experience	45
General interpersonal skills	43
Intercultural interaction skills and experience	28
Political savvy	28
Networking with external stakeholders	17
Mentoring/developing people	13
Counseling, mediation, and conflict resolution	6
Consulting skills and experience	4
Business expertise[a]	85
Intraorganizational expertise	62
Human resources[a]	40
Expertise on external business environment	13
Leadership skills (and experience)	77
Strategic leadership skills and experience	55
General management/leadership skills and experience	36
Organizational improvement/change	21
Project management skills and experience	6
EEO, AA, and diversity knowledge and skills	66
Compliance and legislation	40
Commitment to diversity[b]	32
Knowledge of D&I issues	28

Table B.32—Continued

Codes by Category	% of Interviews ($n = 47$)
Diversity and cultural program experience	19
Personality and attitude[b, c]	64
Driven/motivated	38
Other personality traits	21
Adaptability	17
Organizational skills (conscientiousness)	15
Empathy	15
Integrity	11
Resourceful	2
Personable	2
Analytical abilities and skills	36
Skills involving data and metrics	36
Miscellaneous KSAOs[d]	36
Technical skills or experience	9
Training experience	6
Computer skills	2

[a] For our interviews, we separated business expertise and technical skills. This distinction was not necessary for the job postings, which focus on technical skills. Human resources is under "technical skills or experience" for job postings and is included under "business expertise" for the interviews.

[b] Although we originally coded "commitment to diversity" as part of the category of "EEO, AA, and diversity knowledge and skills," we discuss it in the context of "personality and attitude" because it reflects an attitude, not a knowledge or skill area.

[c] Though it was not included for our interviews, this category also included a "responsible" code for the job postings.

[d] Though they were not included for our interviews, this table also included an "Other KSAOs" category that contained "confidentiality" and "independence" codes for the job postings.

Codes Unique to DoD Interviews

For our DoD interviews, we relied heavily on the codes for the job postings and non-DoD interviews. The codes unique to DoD interviews are shown in Table B.33. As noted at the beginning of this appendix, we do not cite results for DoD interviews because the small sample size could potentially identify individuals by inference.

Table B.33
DoD Interview Codes—Position and Organizational Structure

Category	Coding Descriptions
Position characteristics	
Organization	Air Force, Army, Coast Guard, Marine Corps, National Guard Bureau, and Navy
Leadership level	Senior or non-senior
Diversity office organization and staff requirements	
Compare roles and responsibilities to EO positions	Roles and responsibilities of DoD diversity management leaders are either separate or not separate from those in EO positions.
Compare KSAOs to EO positions	KSAOs needed for DoD diversity management leaders are either the same or not the same as those needed for EO positions.
Reporting structure	Whether a diversity management leader should report to senior leaders in the component.
Personnel mix	Whether a diversity management office should have civilian personnel, military personnel, or both.

Diversity Education Programs

This appendix provides the methodology and results from our review of nine diversity education programs offered by six civilian higher-education institutions. We reviewed the features and content of these programs to complement what we learned about diversity education and training from our interviews with diversity leaders. Our review does not include an exhaustive list of all education programs available to diversity professionals, nor does it evaluate the quality of the programs. Instead, we chose to highlight programs that serve as exemplars. This appendix is intended to be a resource for DoD if it decides to develop policy regarding education requirements for diversity leaders.

Methodology

Program Identification
We used a snowball method to identify diversity education programs. We began with those mentioned by interviewees and then added similar programs found through Internet searches. We chose a convenience sample to highlight well-known programs and only included programs that were active as of fall 2013. To be included, programs had to target individuals in the fields of diversity management and/or EEO and culminate in a degree or certificate. Our sample consists of nine distinct programs run by six different universities. We did not review DoD-run programs.

Content Analysis

We identified key program characteristics of interest, then collected information and created a profile for each program. We gathered descriptive information on the following program characteristics:

- **type:** certificate, master's degree, or other
- **length:** maximum time to complete program and total credits required
- **courses:** courses required, optional courses, and non-course requirements
- **instructional venue:** in person, online, or a mix of in person and online
- **tuition estimate**
- **entry qualifications/criteria:** previous degree, certification, or work experience.

We were particularly interested in the types of courses offered by each program. Where available, we collected and reviewed course descriptions. We then developed a coding framework to describe course content. Courses fell into four broad categories:

- EEO/AA
- diversity
- HR
- skills and practical applications.

Using an iterative process, we further categorized courses into subtopics described later in this appendix. To identify the most common course topics, we tabulated the number and percentage of programs reviewed that included courses in each category.

Program Characteristics

We summarize key characteristics for each program in Table C.1 and discuss them below. Most programs offer a diversity management certificate. Cleveland State University's Diversity Management program is the only one we reviewed that also offers a master's degree. Cornell offers a second level of certification for professionals who have already earned a diversity management certificate. Upon completing the advanced program, participants earn the title of certified diversity professional/advanced practitioner. Cornell also offers an EEO professionals certificate, which was the only EEO-focused program in our sample.

Program venues vary, although most programs offer courses in residence only (i.e., onsite). Rutgers offers its program online or in residence, and Mississippi State University offers its program online only. The tuition estimates vary greatly across programs, from about $3,000 for Cornell's advanced practitioner certificate to $25,000 for Cleveland State University's master's degree program. In summary, three programs cost $5,000 or less, three fell in the $5,000 to $10,000 range, and three exceeded $10,000.

Prerequisites

Most programs target diversity professionals, although there are exceptions. Cleveland State also allows current master's degree students at the university to enroll in its certificate program and welcomes young adults interested in an academic career in D&I to enroll in its master's program. Five of the programs require a bachelor's degree for admission. Two programs have a specific work experience requirement: Cornell's Certified Diversity Professional/Advanced Practitioner (CCDP/AP) program requires three years of experience as a diversity professional, as well as the completion of the Diversity Management Certificate program. The University of Houston's Diversity Management Certificate program requires at least two years of experience in jobs or roles that are related to D&I.

Program Requirements

The requirements for program completion vary greatly. Most programs last between 15 and 24 months. However, the University of Houston's Diversity Management Certificate program can be completed in as few as four and a half days. Most programs require between four and nine courses or workshops. Cleveland State University's master's degree pro-

Table C.1
Program Characteristics

Name	Type	Length (maximum)	Number of Courses/ Workshops Required	Credits Required	Prerequisites (degree)	Venue	Tuition
Cleveland State University, College of Sciences and Health Professions							
Diversity Management Program (DMP): Graduate certificate in diversity management/certification as a diversity professional (CDP)[a]	Certificate	15 months	9 courses	18 credits	Bachelor's	Residence	$18,282
DMP: Master's degree in diversity management/CDP[b]	Master's	21 months	13 courses	40 credits	Bachelor's	Residence	$25,444
Cornell University, School of Industrial and Labor Relations							
Diversity management certificate[c]	Certificate	18 months	6 workshops	72 units	Not specified	Residence	$8,970
Cornell Certified Diversity Professional/Advanced Practitioner (CCDP/AP)[d]	Certificate	18 months	2 courses	18–24 units	Diversity Management Certificate	Residence	$2,985– $3,485
EEO professionals certificate[e]	Certificate	18 months	6 workshops (1 to 3 days each)	72 units	Not specified	Residence	$9,170

Table C.1—Continued

Name	Type	Length (maximum)	Number of Courses/ Workshops Required	Credits Required	Prerequisites (degree)	Venue	Tuition
Georgetown University, School of Continuing Studies: Center for Continuing and Professional Education							
Strategic D&I management[f]	Certificate	24 months	6 courses	10.80 units	Bachelor's	Residence	$5,970
Mississippi State University, College of Arts and Sciences							
Diversity certificate[g]	Certificate	None specified	4 courses	12 credits	Bachelor's	Online	$4,500–$5,000
Rutgers University, School of Management and Labor Relations							
D&I in the workplace certificate (labor and employment certificate)[h]	Certificate	Not specified	4 courses	12 credits	Bachelor's	Residence or online	$10,000–$16,000
University of Houston, Bauer College of Business							
Diversity Management Certificate program[i]	Certificate	4.5 days	Not specified	Not specified	Not specified	Residence	$3,500

NOTE: All information in this table is accurate as of fall 2013.

SOURCES: [a] Cleveland State University (2013b). [b] Cleveland State University (2013a). [c] Cornell University ILR School (2015b). [d] Cornell University ILR School (2015a). [e] Cornell University ILR School (2015c). [f] Georgetown University School of Continuing Studies (2015). [g] Mississippi State University African American Studies (2013). [h] Rutgers School of Management and Labor Relations (2015). [i] Bauer College of Business, University of Houston (2013).

gram has the largest requirement, with 13 courses. It also requires a field practicum and one of three exit options: comprehensive exam, action research project, or thesis. Cornell's CCDP/AP program requires students to complete a project and pass a certification exam.

Course Topics

We divided courses into four broad categories and identified a number of subtopics. Table C.2 includes the description of each broad category and subtopic, as well as the percentage of the nine programs in our sample that offer courses in each topic. Within each category, subtopics are listed in order from most to least common. EEO/AA and diversity were the most common categories and were found in eight out of the nine programs. Courses related to HR and practical skills were found in seven programs.

EEO/AA Courses

Nearly all programs (89 percent) contained EEO/AA courses. We identified three subtopics. The most popular subtopic was law, which was included in 78 percent of the programs. These courses cover EEO and AA laws and issues related to compliance. They may also include content on AA plans. Few programs offered courses with a specific focus on complaints and EEO investigations (33 percent) or harassment and discrimination (22 percent). This is consistent with our understanding that diversity leaders do not usually have responsibilities for compliance but can benefit from a background in EEO and AA. Cornell was the only school to offer a harassment and discrimination workshop, which is described as follows:

> For EEO/HR professionals and managers, prevention is the key to maintaining a productive workplace and avoiding illegal harassment on the job, including sexual, racial, religious, ethnic, age, disability and other types of harassment. This interactive, one-day workshop examines the legal and policy concerns, as well as best practices for creating a workplace of respect and dignity. (Cornell University ILR School, 2015b)

Table C.2
Course Topics and Descriptions

Course Topic and Percentage of Programs Offering	Description
EEO/AA (89%)	Includes any course that covers topics related to EEO or AA.
Law (78%)	Course reviews specific EEO and AA laws, as well as issues related to compliance. May include AA plans.
Complaints/ investigations (33%)	Course addresses formal EEO or harassment complaints and the process of carrying out investigations. May address legal implications and options. May also include strategies to address employee concerns and resolve conflict.
Harassment/ discrimination (22%)	Course addresses how to prevent and address harassment and discrimination in the workplace. May address relevant laws.
Diversity (89%)	Includes general issues related to diversity. May include a broad introduction to the field.
Diversity theory and history (67%)	Course reviews the history of the diversity field and related theories from other disciplines (e.g. sociology, psychology, business). May address national and international demographic trends to understand the need for diversity strategies. May also distinguish diversity from EEO and consider the "business case" for diversity.
Change management/ diversity initiatives and strategy (56%)	Course discusses diversity initiatives and strategies, including how they relate to organizational change management. May address specific theories of organizational change.
Managing diversity groups (44%)	Course reviews different types of diversity groups (e.g., affinity groups, diversity councils) and presents strategies for effective management of those groups. May address the rationale for establishing such groups.
Topics tied to subgroups (33%)	Course addresses D&I issues related to specific population subgroups (e.g., women, older workers, immigrants) and how to best accommodate different groups in the workplace. May include a historic review of barriers that particular subgroups have faced.
Other diversity (33%)	Course includes diversity-related topics that go beyond or do not fit neatly in the categories listed above.
Supplier diversity (22%)	Course overviews the purpose and design of supplier diversity programs.

Table C.2—Continued

Course Topic and Percentage of Programs Offering	Description
HR (78%)	Includes any course that covers human resources topics. Courses are generally connected to diversity and EEO issues.
Recruiting/ staffing (78%)	Course reviews strategies for recruiting and managing a diverse staff.
Retention (78%)	Course reviews strategies for retaining a diverse staff. May address ways to maintain an inclusive workplace environment and improve employee satisfaction.
Training and professional development (44%)	Course addresses topics and strategies related to diversity training. May address different training techniques and topics.
Skills and practical applications (78%)	Course addresses soft and hard skills relevant to diversity practitioners and may provide the opportunity for students to practice applying those skills. These skills may include communication, metrics and data analysis, group facilitation, budgeting, leadership, and others.

The only program that did not have a course in EEO or AA was Georgetown's Strategic Diversity and Inclusion Management program.

Diversity Courses

The most popular subtopic in the diversity courses is theory and history, offered by two-thirds of our sample. These courses review the history of the diversity field and related theories from other disciplines and may also address relevant national and international demographic trends. An example of a course that falls into this subtopic is Georgetown's course titled "Foundations of Diversity and Inclusion Management." The course description is as follows:

> This course offers perspective on the historical and sociological factors impacting diversity and inclusion in the U.S. as well as impact on business strategy. It will differentiate between Equal Employment Opportunity (EEO) and affirmative action, and diversity and inclusion. Participants will explore the changing

demographics in the U.S. and the world, and will begin to outline the business case for Diversity and Inclusion and the need for cultural competence. (Georgetown University School of Continuing Studies, 2015)

The only program that did not require a general diversity course was Cornell's EEO professionals certificate program.

The majority of programs (56 percent) had at least one course related to change management or diversity initiatives and strategy. These courses cover general business models in the context of the diversity field. Cleveland State offers a course in diversity and organizational change, described as follows:

This course provides an overview of organizational change models. Discusses the dynamics and complexity of organizational change efforts and gives special attention to addressing organizational resistance. Theories of change management are applied to diversity issues. (Cleveland State University, 2013b)

Many programs (44 percent) offer courses related to the specific topic of managing diversity groups, such as employee resource groups or affinity groups. Cornell offers a course called "Effective Affinity Groups" with the following description:

The benefits of this employee resource group provide a forum in which members of an organization who share common interests, issues or concerns meet to address the impact upon recruitment, retention, marketing and customer relations. (Cornell University ILR School, 2015b)

Only one-third of programs offer courses focusing on specific population subgroups, such as women or immigrants. The least common courses offered are those on supplier diversity. Only the two Cornell diversity programs offered supplier diversity courses.

HR Courses

Most programs included at least one course on an HR topic. While diversity leaders may not be primarily responsible for HR functions, they may be involved with some HR-related activities, such as recruitment and retention. Seventy-eight percent of the programs in our sample offer courses related to recruitment and staffing. For example, Georgetown has a course called "Recruitment, Retention, Resistance, Renewal: Managing Change." The program's website describes this course as a "systems approach to managing diversity and inclusion in the workplace" that covers the following content:

> Participants will review best practices, benchmarks, standards, and current research on global diversity and inclusion to learn how best to recruit and retain a diverse talent pool. The difference between a diverse and an inclusive workplace will be probed, as well as the roles that resistance and conflict play in any change effort, especially those dealing with workplace differences. (Georgetown University School of Continuing Studies, 2015)

Rutgers offers a course on professional development strategies that reviews best practices related to retention and training. Four programs have courses on leading diversity training. The University of Houston's course covers the rationale for diversity training, types of training, and related barriers and challenges. The only programs that do not include HR courses are Mississippi State University's diversity certificate programs and Cornell's EEO professionals certificate program.

Skills and Practical Applications
Many programs have a practicum component. We defined this category to include courses that address soft and hard skills relevant to diversity practitioners and that may provide the opportunity for students to practice applying those skills. These skills may include communication, metrics and data analysis, group facilitation, budgeting, and leadership, among others. Not surprisingly, these topics match many of the KSAOs identified by our interviewees as important for diversity leaders. Georgetown's skills course is titled "Leading for Innovation and Inclusion," and its course description is as follows:

> This course will cover the use of effective communication skills such as giving and receiving feedback, and the art of influenc-

ing and empowering others, to examine the subtle differences between managing and leading cultural and diversity initiatives. The course will serve as a general overview of the four courses that have preceded it through a leadership lens. (Georgetown University School of Continuing Studies, 2015)

The only programs that did not include this component were those offered by Mississippi State University and Rutgers University.

References

Abrami, Philip C., Robert M. Bernard, Evgueni Borokhovski, Anne Wade, Michael A. Surkes, Rana Tamim, and Dai Zhang, "Instructional Interventions Affecting Critical Thinking Skills and Dispositions: A Stage 1 Meta-Analysis," *Review of Educational Research*, Vol. 78, No. 4, 2008, pp. 1102–1134.

Agresti, Alan, *An Introduction to Categorical Data Analysis*, New York: Wiley, 1996.

American Hospital Association Institute for Diversity in Health Management and Association of American Medical Colleges, *The Role of the Chief Diversity Officer in Academic Health Centers*, November 2012. As of April 8, 2013:
https://members.aamc.org/eweb/upload/
The%20Role%20of%20the%20Chief%20Diversity%20Officer%20in%20
Academic%20Health%20Centers.pdf

Avolio, Bruce J., John J. Sosik, Dong I. Jung, and Yair Berson, "Leadership Models, Methods, and Applications," in Walter C. Borman, Daniel R. Ilgen, and Richard J. Klimoski, eds., *Handbook of Psychology, Volume 12: Industrial and Organizational Psychology*, Hoboken, N.J.: Wiley & Sons, 2003, pp. 277–307.

Bauer College of Business, University of Houston, "The 'Diversity Management Certificate' Program," 2013. As of March 11, 2015:
http://bauer.uh.edu/degrees-programs/certificates/diversity-management.php

Brannick, Michael T., Edward L. Levine, and Frederick P. Morgeson, *Job and Work Analysis: Methods, Research, and Applications for Human Resource Management*, 2nd ed., Thousand Oaks, Calif.: Sage Publications, 2007.

Chrobot-Mason, Donna, "Developing Multicultural Competence for Managers: Same Old Leadership Skills or Something New?" *The Psychologist-Manager Journal*, Vol. 6, No. 2, 2003, pp. 5–20.

Cleveland State University, "Diversity Management Specialization M.A.," 2013a. As of March 11, 2015:
https://www.csuohio.edu/sciences/diversity_management/node/2726

Cleveland State University, "Diversity Management Specialization M.A.: Graduate Certificate Information," 2013b. As of March 11, 2015:
https://www.csuohio.edu/sciences/diversity_management/
graduate-certificate-information

Cohen, Debra, Society for Human Resources Management, "Implementing Diversity and Inclusion Practice in Organizations: Challenges and Opportunities," discussant on panel presentation at the 30th Annual Conference of the Society for Industrial and Organizational Psychology, Philadelphia, Pa., April 25, 2015.

Connelly, Mary S., Jannelle A. Gilbert, Stephen J. Zaccaro, K. Victoria Threlfall, Michelle A. Marks, and Michael D. Mumford, "Exploring the Relationship of Leadership Skills and Knowledge to Leader Performance," *Leadership Quarterly*, Vol. 11, No. 1, 2000, pp. 65–86.

Cornell University ILR School, "Certification (CCDP/AP): Cornell Certified Diversity Professional/Advanced Practitioner (CCDP/AP)," 2015a. As of March 11, 2015:
http://www.ilr.cornell.edu/hcd/certificates/dm/cdp.html

———, "Diversity and Inclusion Professionals Certificate," 2015b. As of March 11, 2015:
http://www.ilr.cornell.edu/hcd/certificates/dm/diversityManagement.html

———, "EEO Professionals Certificate," 2015c. As of March 11, 2015:
http://www.ilr.cornell.edu/hcd/certificates/eeo/eeoStudies.html

Cox, Taylor, Jr., and Ruby L. Beale, *Developing Competency to Manage Diversity: Readings, Cases & Activities*, San Francisco, Calif.: Berrett-Koehler Publishers, 1997.

Curtis, Ellen Foster, and Janice L. Dreachslin, "Diversity Management Interventions and Organizational Performance: A Synthesis of Current Literature," *Human Resource Development Review*, Vol. 7, No. 1, 2008, pp. 107–134.

Dexter, Billy, "The Chief Diversity Officer Today: Inclusion Gets Down to Business," Chicago, Ill.: Heidrick & Struggles, March 8, 2010, pp. 1–8.

DoD—*see* U.S. Department of Defense.

DoDD—*see* U.S. Department of Defense Directive.

Galanaki, Eleanna, Dimitris Bourantas, and Nancy Papalexandris, "A Decision Model for Outsourcing Training Functions: Distinguishing Between Generic and Firm-Job-Specific Training Content," *The International Journal of Human Resource Management*, Vol. 19, No. 12, 2008, pp. 2332–2351.

Georgetown University School of Continuing Studies, "Strategic Diversity and Inclusion Management," 2015. As of March 11, 2015:
http://scs.georgetown.edu/programs_nc/CE0050/
strategic-diversity-and-inclusion-management?dId=5

Gibbons, Alyssa M., Deborah E. Rupp, Lori A. Snyder, A. Silke Holub, and Sang Eun Woo, "A Preliminary Investigation of Developable Dimensions," *The Psychologist-Manager Journal*, Vol. 9, No. 2, 2006, pp. 99–123.

Halpern, Diane F., "The Development of Adult Cognition: Understanding Constancy and Change in Adult Learning," in David V. Day, Stephen J. Zaccaro, and Stanley M. Halpern, eds., *Leader Development for Transforming Organizations: Growing Leaders for Tomorrow*, Mahwah, N.J.: Lawrence Erlbaum Associates, 2004, pp. 125–152.

Hays-Thomas, Rosemary, and Marc Bendick, Jr., "Professionalizing Diversity and Inclusion Practice: Should Voluntary Standards be the Chicken or the Egg?" *Industrial and Organizational Psychology*, Vol. 6, No. 3, 2013, pp. 193–205.

Hays-Thomas, Rosemary, Alyinth Bowen, and Megan Boudreaux, "Skills for Diversity and Inclusion in Organizations: A Review and Preliminary Investigation," *The Psychologist-Manager Journal*, Vol. 15, 2012, pp. 128–141.

Hogan, Robert, and Robert B. Kaiser, "What We Know About Leadership," *Journal of General Psychology*, Vol. 9, No. 2, 2005, pp. 169–180.

Hogan, Robert, and Rodney Warrenfeltz, "Educating the Modern Manager," *Academy of Management Learning and Education*, Vol. 2, No. 1, 2003, pp. 74–84.

Holvino, Evangelina, Bernardo M. Ferdman, and Deborah Merrill-Sands, "Creating and Sustaining Diversity and Inclusion in Organizations: Strategies and Approaches," in Margaret S. Stockdale and Faye J. Crosby, eds., *The Psychology and Management of Workplace Diversity*, Malden, Mass.: Blackwell, 2004, pp. 245–276.

Klein, Cameron Robert, *What Do We Know About Interpersonal Skills? A Meta-Analytic Examination of Antecedents, Outcomes, and the Efficacy of Training*, dissertation, 2009, Orlando, Fla.: University of Central Florida, Dissertation Abstracts International: Section B: The Sciences and Engineering, Vol. 70(5-B), 2009.

Kulik, Carol T., and Loriann Roberson, "Common Goals and Golden Opportunities: Evaluations of Diversity Education in Academic and Organization Settings," *Academy of Management Learning and Education*, Vol. 7, No. 3, 2008, pp. 309–331.

Lahiri, Indra, *Creating a Competency Model for Diversity and Inclusion Practitioners*, New York: The Conference Board Council on Workforce Diversity, CP-005, 2008. As of December 10, 2012:
http://www.conference-board.org/pdf_free/councils/TCBCP005.pdf

Leibrecht, Bruce C., David H. McGilvray, Douglas L. Tystad, and Sena Garven, *Operational Assessment of Tools for Accelerating Leader Development (ALD): Volume 1, Capstone Report*, Arlington, Va.: U.S. Army Research Institute for the Behavioral and Social Sciences, Technical Report 1252, June 2009.

Mayer, John D., Peter Salovey, and David R. Caruso, "Emotional Intelligence: New Ability or Eclectic Traits?" *American Psychologist,* Vol. 63, No. 6, 2008, pp. 503–517.

Military Leadership Diversity Commission, *Military Leadership Diversity Commission Decision Paper #6: Diversity Leadership,* Arlington, Va., February 2011.

Mississippi State University African American Studies, "Diversity Certificate Program," 2013. As of March 11, 2015:
http://www.aas.msstate.edu/program/certificate.php

Mumford, Michael D., Michael A. Campion, and Frederick P. Morgeson, "The Leadership Skills Strataplex: Leadership Skill Requirements Across Organizational Levels," *The Leadership Quarterly,* Vol. 18, No. 2, 2007, pp. 154–166.

Mumford, Michael D., Stephen J. Zaccaro, Francis D. Harding, T. Owen Jacobs, and Edwin A. Fleishman, "Leadership Skills for a Changing World: Solving Complex Social Problems," *Leadership Quarterly,* Vol. 11, No. 1, 2000, pp. 11–35.

OPM—*see* U.S. Office of Personnel Management.

Roberts, Brent W., Kate E. Walton, and Wolfgang Viechtbauer, "Patterns of Mean-Level Change in Personality Traits Across the Life Course: A Meta-Analysis of Longitudinal Studies," *Psychological Bulletin,* Vol. 132, No. 1, 2006, pp. 1–25.

Rosete, David, *Does Emotional Intelligence Play an Important Role in Leadership Effectiveness?* thesis, University of Wollongong, Wollongong, New South Wales, Australia, 2007.

Rupp, Deborah E., Lori A. Snyder, Alyssa M. Gibbons, and George C. Thornton III, "What Should Developmental Assessment Centers Be Developing?" *The Psychologist-Manager Journal,* Vol. 9, No. 2, 2006, pp. 75–98.

Rutgers School of Management and Labor Relations, "Diversity and Inclusion in the Workplace Certificate," 2015. As of March 11, 2015:
http://smlr.rutgers.edu/labor-and-employment-relations/DiversityInclusion

Sackett, Paul S., and Roxanne M. Laczo, "Job and Work Analysis," in Walter C. Borman, Daniel R. Ilgen, and Richard J. Klimoski, eds., *Handbook of Psychology: Volume 12, Industrial and Organizational Psychology,* Hoboken, N.J.: John Wiley & Sons, 2003, pp. 21–37.

Sanchez, Juan I., and Edward L. Levine, "What Is (or Should Be) the Differences Between Competency Modeling and Traditional Job Analysis?" *Human Resource Management Review,* Vol. 19, 2009, pp. 53–63.

Shore, Lynn M., Amy E. Randel, Beth G. Chung, Michelle A. Dean, Karen Holcombe Ehrhart, and Gangaram Singh, "Inclusion and Diversity in Work Groups: A Review and Model for Future Research," *Journal of Management,* Vol. 37, No. 4, 2011, pp. 1262–1289.

Thornton, George C., III, and William C. Byham, *Assessment Centers and Managerial Performance*, New York: Academic Press, 1982.

Thornton, George C., III, and Deborah E. Rupp, *Assessment Centers in Human Resource Management*, Mahwah, N.J.: Lawrence Erlbaum, 2005.

U.S. Department of Defense, *Diversity and Inclusion Strategic Plan: 2012–2017*, 2012. As of February 11, 2013:
http://diversity.defense.gov/Portals/51/Documents/
DoD_Diversity_Strategic_Plan_%20final_as%20of%2019%20Apr%2012[1].pdf

U.S. Department of Defense Directive 1020.02, "Diversity Management and Equal Opportunity (EO) in the Department of Defense," Washington, D.C.: U.S. Department of Defense, Under Secretary of Defense for Personnel and Readiness, February 5, 2009.

U.S. Department of Defense Directive 1350.2, "Department of Defense Military Equal Opportunity (MEO) Program," Washington, D.C.: U.S. Department of Defense, Under Secretary of Defense for Personnel and Readiness, August 18, 1995.

U.S. Office of Personnel Management, Office of Diversity and Inclusion, *Government-Wide Diversity and Inclusion Strategic Plan*, 2011.

Visagie, Jan, Herman Linde, and Werner Havenga, "Leadership Competencies for Managing Diversity," *Managing Global Transitions*, Vol. 9, No. 3, 2011, pp. 225–247.

White House, "Executive Order 13583—Establishing a Coordinated Government-Wide Initiative to Promote Diversity and Inclusion in the Federal Workforce," Washington, D.C., August 18, 2011. As of February 3, 2016:
https://www.whitehouse.gov/the-press-office/2011/08/18/
executive-order-13583-establishing-coordinated-government-wide-initiativ

Williams, Damon A., and Katrina C. Wade-Golden, "The Chief Diversity Officer," *CUPA-HR Journal*, Vol. 58, No. 1, 2007, pp. 38–48.

Zaccaro, Stephen J., Cary Kemp, and Paige Bader, "Leader Traits and Attributes," *The Nature of Leadership*, Vol. 101, 2004, pp. 101–124.